VICTIMS OF BENEVOLENCE

VICTIMS OF BENEVOLENCE

THE DARK LEGACY OF
THE WILLIAMS LAKE RESIDENTIAL SCHOOL

Elizabeth Furniss

ARSENAL PULP PRESS
Vancouver

VICTIMS OF BENEVOLENCE
Copyright © 1992 and 1995 by the Cariboo Tribal Council

Third printing: 2011

ARSENAL PULP PRESS
#101-211 East Georgia St.
Vancouver, BC
Canada V6A 1Z6
arsenalpulp.com

The publisher gratefully acknowledges the support of the Canada Council for the Arts and the British Columbia Arts Council for its publishing program, and the Government of Canada through the Canada Book Fund and the Government of British Columbia through the Book Publishing Tax Credit Program for its publishing activities.

Printed and bound in Canada

Library and Archives Canada Cataloguing in Publication

Furniss, Elizabeth, 1959-
Victims of benevolence

Includes bibliographical references.

ISBN 978-1-55152-015-5

1. Cariboo Tribal Council—History.   2. Shuswap Indians—Residential schools—History.★   3. Indians of North America—British Columbia—Williams Lake—Residential Schools—History.★   4. Indians, Treatment of—British Columbia—Williams Lake—History.   1. Title

E96.6W54F87 1994   371.97'979   C94-910729-8

The Indians, being nomadic by nature, wish to be free to come and go as they please. It is not surprising, therefore, that their children found the confinement and discipline of school life hard to bear, and that, consequently, several of them ran away. One of these, a young boy, was found dead in the woods. To pacify his parents and the other Indians was no easy task. It was difficult also to persuade the Indians to send their children to school and to keep them there all during the school term. This took a great deal of diplomacy on the part of the Principals and the Sisters. As for the missionary, he spent hours and hours on the various reservations trying to persuade the Indians to send their children to school and to return to the school those who had run away.

—Father Francois Marie Thomas, O.M.I., *Memoirs*

Contents

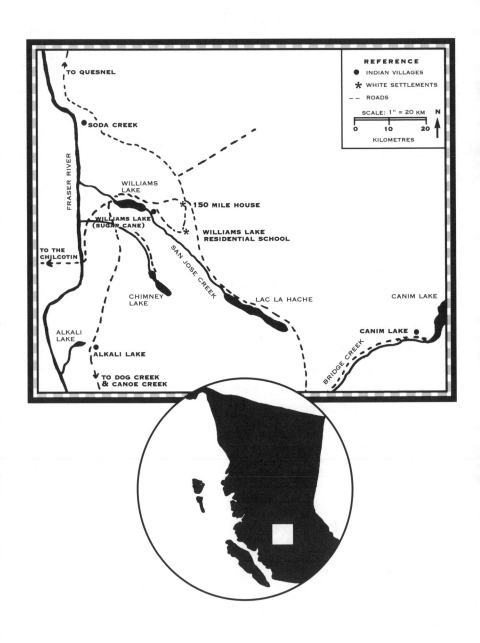

REFERENCE
● INDIAN VILLAGES
✱ WHITE SETTLEMENTS
-- ROADS

SCALE: 1" = 20 KM

0   10   20
KILOMETRES

N

TO QUESNEL

● SODA CREEK

FRASER RIVER

WILLIAMS
LAKE

✱ 150 MILE HOUSE

WILLIAMS LAKE
(SUGAR CANE)

TO THE
CHILCOTIN

✱ WILLIAMS LAKE
RESIDENTIAL SCHOOL

SAN JOSE CREEK

CHIMNEY
LAKE

LAC LA HACHE

CANIM LAKE

CANIM LAKE ●

ALKALI
LAKE

● ALKALI LAKE

BRIDGE CREEK

↓ TO DOG CREEK
& CANOE CREEK

Preface

THIS PROJECT BEGAN IN 1990, when I was asked by the Cariboo Tribal Council of Williams Lake, British Columbia, to draw together some general information on the history of St. Joseph's residential school, known locally as the Mission. I was approached to do this research because of my previous working relationship as an aboriginal rights co-ordinator with the Council, and because of my familiarity with the archival sources of information on the Shuswap and the early missionaries to the Cariboo. This study was one component of a broader research program undertaken by the Cariboo Tribal Council to assess the long term psychological and social impacts of the residential schools on their communities.[1]

In my review of federal files which contain administrative records and correspondence of the Department of Indian and Northern Affairs, I found a wealth of documents—primarily letters and inquest affidavits—discussing problems in the care being provided to students at the school during the early years of the school's operation. On the basis of these documents, I wrote a preliminary report for the Tribal Council chiefs, a report entitled *A Conspiracy of Silence: The Care of Native Students at St. Joseph's Residential School, Williams Lake, B.C.* In 1992 I rewrote this study as a booklet for readers among the fifteen Shuswap, Carrier, and Chilcotin communities. The booklet was published by the Cariboo Tribal Council under the title *Victims of Benevolence: Discipline and Death at the Williams Lake Indian Residential School, 1891-1920.* Many people from the Shuswap, Chilcotin, and Carrier nations attended the Mission, and all have their own stories to tell about life at the school. Virtually none of the past students I have spoken with have been surprised at the events described here. A number have said that the events documented here are simply "the tip of the iceberg."

The stories of the tragic deaths of two young boys at St. Joseph's Mission, the subsequent government investigations, and the responses of the Oblates and government officials now are retold here for a broader, more general audience. I have expanded the text to provide more background information on government policy, the residential school system, and current discourse on the residential school issue. These stories have been retold here in the belief that they have much relevance to current discussions of the impact of the residential schools on First Nations in Canada. While the residential schools have now closed, the relationships that existed between First Nations, the church, and the government, relationships that are central to this story, still persist today.

This story has been reconstructed from information contained in archival documents. I have chosen to use archival sources not because I believe they are any more "objective" than oral traditions and personal accounts; on the contrary, it is now generally accepted, within contemporary anthropology, that written documents do not contain objective truths, but provide subjective information shaped by the cultural biases and perspectives of their authors.[2] In most cases, historical records have been written by non-Natives and thus reflect a non-Native cultural orientation. As a result, Native perspectives are often excluded from documentary sources of information, making it critical, especially when researching such contentious issues as the history and impact of the Indian residential school system, to consult Native people for information based on their first-hand experiences and oral traditions. The set of archival documents that I draw on here, however, is unusual in that Native voices have been very well documented in the form of affidavits and letters. From these documents Native voices emerge loudly and clearly, and they deserve to be honoured.

At the same time, it was not through these documents that I was first introduced to the residential school issue. For several years previous, in the course of working with the Cariboo Tribal Council and developing friendships with First Nations people, I had heard many stories of peoples' experiences at the Mission. I was present in the area when the first Oblate from St. Joseph's Mission was charged with sex-related crimes, and when the residential school topic emerged as a critical issue of discussion within the local Native communities. These experiences, plus my engagement with the scholarly literature on Native-white relations in the course of doctoral studies in anthropology at the University of British Columbia, have significantly shaped my understanding of the impact of the residential schools on First Nations people and communities.

I would like to thank the past and present Chiefs of the Cariboo Tribal Council—William Alphonse Jr., Antoine Archie, Bill Chelsea, Gabriel (Roy) Christopher, Rick

Gilbert, Bev Sellars, Lenny Sellars, and Agnes Snow—as well as Charlene Belleau, past social development co-ordinator with the Cariboo Tribal Council, and Bruce Mack, acting Tribal Council administrator, for giving me the opportunity to research and write this study. Thanks also go to Sharon Bob of the Cariboo Tribal Council for all her administrative work and her help with pulling together old photographs. I'd also like to thank Julie Cruikshank, who provided critical feedback on an earlier draft, and Renee Richards and Michael Barnholden, who supported and promoted this book in its earlier version.

This book represents not the Cariboo Tribal Council's, but my own perspective of the residential school issue. The names of the two boys have been used in consultation with their families. The royalties from the sales of this book will go towards educational bursaries for First Nations students of the Cariboo region.

CHAPTER ONE

A "Sacred Duty":
Christianity, Civilization,
and Indian Education

THIS BOOK IS ABOUT the first three decades in the life of an Indian residential school in the central interior of British Columbia. It is about a dream shared by the Roman Catholic missionaries and the Canadian government: to see Native people, through residential schooling, abandon their cultural heritage and their nomadic hunting and fishing lifestyle, and adopt the presumably civilized ways of Europeans. With Native people living as whites, wearing European dress, speaking the English language, and working as farmers or labourers within the colonial economy, the "Indian problem," government and church agents believed, would no longer exist: Indians would meld seamlessly into the mainstream society.

It was a grandiose and fatal plan, and as the Oblates of St. Joseph's Mission soon were to find, one not easily accomplished. The Shuswap people of the Williams Lake area accepted the Roman Catholic missionaries and the residential school program only reluctantly. Throughout the first thirty years of the school's operation, Native people, at times indirectly, at other times openly and vigorously, struggled against the assimilation plan, the residential school program, and the Oblates' control over their children's lives. These simmering tensions between the Native population, church agents, and government officials were drawn to a head by the tragic deaths of two young students at the Mission school, one in 1902, the other in 1920.

The first death was that of Duncan Sticks. Born in 1893 to the family of Johnny Sticks of Alkali Lake, Duncan had been taken to the Indian residential school near Williams Lake at an early age. He was unhappy at the school, and on a February afternoon in 1902, Duncan and eight other boys ran away. While the other boys eventually were captured and returned to the school, Duncan disappeared into the forest. His body was found the next day by a local rancher; Duncan had died by the roadside thirteen kilometers from the school.

The second death was that of a young boy named Augustine Allan from Canim Lake. Augustine committed suicide while at the residential school in the summer of 1920. He and eight other boys had made a suicide pact and had gathered together to eat poisonous water hemlock. Augustine died, but the other eight survived.

The deaths of these two boys raised many important questions and drew critical public scrutiny to the plight of students at the Mission. Why did these boys die? What was happening at the school? Why were children running away, or attempting suicide?

The early history of the St. Joseph's Mission school, and the deaths of Duncan Sticks and Augustine Allan, are recounted in the following pages. These stories are told here in the belief that they evoke issues that are essential to an understanding of contemporary discussions of the Indian residential schools and their impact on First Nations in

Canada.[1] Yet this is not simply the story of the deaths of two young boys, or even of the Indian residential school system. More importantly, the events portrayed in this book reveal how the long-term structural relationship between First Nations and the Canadian government, and the beliefs that have legitimized this relationship, have had tragic consequences for innocent people.

COLONIAL POLICY
AND THE IMAGE OF THE INDIAN

Indian residential schools were the product of the nineteenth-century federal policy of assimilation. To understand how and why this policy was created, we must look deeper into the history of Indian-white relations, and to the beliefs that Europeans have held about Indian people since the Europeans' first arrival in North America.

Over the last four centuries, two fundamental assumptions have characterized the dominant attitudes held by Europeans towards Indians in North America. First, Europeans have presumed their society to be inherently superior to that of Native peoples, not only in terms of technology but in terms of moral, intellectual, and artistic development. Native peoples have been perceived not as existing in complex societies, having their own systems of government, their own social and political institutions, and their own highly-developed technologies and intellectual and artistic traditions, but as a child-like, savage race, having only a rudimentary degree of social organization, living a precarious, hand-to-mouth existence, and adhering to superstitious, pagan beliefs. Second, following this premise of superiority, Europeans have taken it upon themselves, to varying degrees in different historical periods, to transform Native peoples, both physically and culturally, into an image more acceptable to European sensibilities. This effort has been legitimized by a fundamental conviction that Native people require the guidance of Europeans to live successful lives, and that European intervention in Native peoples' lives, even when forcefully applied, is ultimately in Native peoples' 'best interests.'

Of all groups within colonial society, Christian missionaries have been the most consistent in adopting roles of paternalistic benefactors to Native communities, and in seeking to transform Indians into European ideals. The impulse to convert people to the Christian faith was not unique to missionary relations with North American Native peoples. From its inception Christianity has been an evangelical movement, driven by Jesus' final words of advice to his disciples: "Go therefore and make disciples of all nations, baptizing them in the name of the Father and of the Son and of the Holy Spirit, teaching them to observe all that I have commanded you."[2] The belief that the salvation of one's soul depended on the acceptance of Christian faith, and that the second coming of Christ would occur only when the gospel had spread through the world, were common long before European arrival in North America.[3] Armed with these convictions, the first missionaries to arrive on the shores of New France in the seventeenth century imagined the New World as an untouched territory, one ripe for the missionary teachings and one in which they could prove their devotion to their faith through their heroic self-sacrifice.

From the outset, and with the full support of both the French monarchy and its colonial officials, the Roman Catholic missionaries to New France saw their task as not only to

Christianize, but to civilize Native peoples into the dress, language, and habits of French culture.[4] By the early 1600s Jesuit and Recollet missionaries had begun to preach the gospel to the Micmac, Montagnais, Algonquin, and Huron nations in a territory stretching from the Gulf of St. Lawrence to Georgian Bay. The education of Natives in church-run schools, where feasible, was a central component of the missionary plan. By the 1630s the Jesuits had built a residential school for Huron children at Quebec City, and had established a mission where they were encouraging the nearby Montagnais to settle into agricultural villages.[5]

With the fall of New France and the establishment of British sovereignty in the next century, a path was cleared for the expansion of other Christian denominations, notably Anglican and Methodist, into Upper Canada. In the following decades Anglican, Methodist, and Roman Catholic missionaries spread further westward and northward across the continent, competing amongst each other for influence and favour among the various Native nations. By the mid-1800s most regions of Canada had been claimed by particular religious denominations. In British Columbia, Roman Catholic missions were established throughout the interior, while Anglican and Methodist missionaries vied for territory on the northern coast. All three denominations, and the Presbyterian church, were active in the more heavily settled regions on the south coast and Vancouver Island.

Not all groups within colonial society had the same motives for entering into relationships with Native peoples, nor did they always share the same vision of how Native people should live their lives. The political and economic interests of fur traders, settlers, and government officials at times complemented, and at times conflicted with, the missionary -

program. For example, missionaries and fur traders often worked closely together. Missionaries typically arrived in new territories with the fur brigades, and depended heavily on company employees for food, assistance, and introductions to the Native nations. While fur traders shared the prevalent beliefs of the time about the primitiveness of Native cultures, they were willing to tolerate what they saw as barbaric customs and practices in order to maintain good business relations. The success of the fur trade was conditional on Native people continuing to occupy their lands and practice their traditional pursuits of hunting, fishing, and trapping. Further, traders perceived disruptions to the integrity of Native communities to be potential threats to the continued success of the enterprise. Because of these conflicting interests and their dependence on the fur traders, missionaries at times were forced to temper the civilizing component of their mandate.[6]

For their part, government officials ultimately were concerned with maintaining their authority within the colonies, with ensuring the safety of settlers, and with facilitating the expansion of an agricultural and industrial economy. Through the 17th and 18th centuries Native nations played critical roles as military allies in the wars between the British and the French. For the sake of maintaining these strategic alliances, colonial administrators were reluctant to interfere too drastically in the lives of Native peoples and communities. As a result, for much of the period leading up to Canadian confederation, both the French and later the British colonial governments followed a general policy of conciliation towards aboriginal peoples.[7] In practice, this policy translated into a variety of initiatives for relating to Native nations, initiatives that were shaped by local conditions and pragmatic concerns.[8] Government agents were content with allowing missionaries to assume the role of front line agents of paternalism. Missionary endeavours were supported, both financially and morally, as long as they were received favourably by the Native communities and did not incite radical social change.[9]

With the establishment of British colonial authority in 1760, the conclusion of the War of 1812, and the rapid expansion of white settlement westward, Indian-European relations shifted from ones of strategic partnership to ones of direct, open competition for land and resources. Indians now were viewed as obstacles to the country's development. In regions of intense Indian-white conflicts over land, settlers began to generate racist discourses and calls for government assistance in suppressing the Indian populations. In the most heavily settled regions, Native populations were becoming destitute and overwhelmed by the effects of epidemics, social upheaval, and economic dislocation from their traditional lands. Where Indians were no longer perceived as a threat, the settler population could afford feelings of sympathy; the hostile savage image gave way to the image of the Indian as the noble savage to be pitied and protected. This image gained widespread popularity among the Canadian public in the first half of the 1800s through the historical romances of Fennimore Cooper and the paintings of George Caitlin and Paul Kane, and through later travel narratives by such writers as William Francis Butler and George Grant, all of whom lamented the vanishing of the Indian race.[10]

Such concerns for the welfare of Native people were a reflection of a more general humanitarian ideology that arose through the social reform movements of the early 1800s in Britain and the U.S. The industrial revolution in Britain had brought with it a dislocation of the population from rural to urban centers as well as critical disparities in wealth between socio-economic classes. The low wages, bad working conditions, and urban ghettos in which many of the poor were forced to live became key issues through which liberal politicians, missionaries, and labour spokesmen launched their public critiques. Similar calls for social and economic reforms arose as the industrial economy expanded in the early 19th-century United States. These general public concerns with issues of poverty and social conditions were extended to the plight of Native Indians; public pressure in Canada began to be applied on missionaries and colonial officials to provide Native communities with aid and assistance.[11]

The intersection of political and economic interests, missionary ideology, and popular humanitarianism laid the foundation for the transformation of the policy of conciliation to a policy of civilization in Canada during the early 1800s. In contrast, British colonial officials now sought to directly intervene in Native communities and to encourage Natives to adopt the civilized practices and habits of European society. The first government-initiated civilization strategy was enacted in Upper Canada in the 1830s.[12] With the collaboration of Methodist missionaries, a program was developed to establish permanent villages and schools where Natives would be settled and taught basic literacy, agricultural, and industrial trades, as well as principles of Christian morality and belief. The ultimate goal of this program was to create Christianized, civilized, and self-governing Native communities under the protection of the British government.[13] The program had the additional benefit of ensuring that adjacent lands once occupied by Native peoples would now be free for white settlement.

Despite initial difficulties, over the next decades Method-ist, Anglican, and Roman Catholic churches, with state sup-port and funding, continued in their ventures to civilize Native populations. Education increasingly became viewed as the most effective means of bringing this about, and schools began to be established throughout the most heavily settled regions where Native peoples were most destitute. By the 1850s the program of civilization through education in church-run schools had been firmly entrenched in the mis-sionary tradition throughout Canada.

Through the history of Indian-white relations in Canada, Native peoples have sought to mold and manipulate their relationships with missionaries, fur traders, and government agents in order to advance their own interests. In many regions Native peoples initially supported the establishment of missionary-run schools, believing that a knowledge of the English language and agricultural and trade skills would enhance their opportunities, while at the same time enabling them to maintain their communities and their traditional cultures in their changing economic circumstances. This had been the hope of the Native nations of Upper Canada when the first industrial schools had been established in the 1830s. Yet by the 1860s support for Christianity and mission educa-tion in Upper Canada was diminishing, as tribal councils rejected the mission program as one geared to dividing their communities and dismantling their cultures.[14]

As Native resistance mounted, missionaries and govern-ment agents began to adopt more coercive measures to encourage the civilization of Native peoples. The paternalis-tic presumption that missionaries and government agents had long used to justify their relationships with Native people— that they were working in Natives' 'best interests'—now began to be expressed through the creation of a coercive federal Indian policy which sought not only to civilize, but to forcibly assimilate Indians into the dominant, Euro-Canadian society.[15]

FEDERAL INDIAN POLICY

In 1867 the federal government of Canada, through the terms of the British North America Act, took on the official responsibility for managing Indians and Indian lands. Native people continued to be seen by Euro-Canadians as a child-like, primitive, and inferior race. These assumptions now were encoded in legislation, as Native peoples were legally defined as non-citizens and wards of the state. Federal Indian policy explicitly sought to protect Native peoples in isolated reserve communities, where they would be sheltered from white encroachment and from the immoral influences of the rougher side of white frontier culture, and where Indians could be subject to government efforts to steer them into a process of cultural change. Existing Indian laws in 1876 were consolidated into legislation known as the Indian Act, which provided government representatives with sweeping powers to control and direct virtually every aspect of Native lives.

By 1880 a separate government agency, later known as the Department of Indian Affairs, was set up to administer federal Indian policy.[16] The highest position within the bureaucracy was the office of the Deputy Superintendent General of Indian Affairs, stationed in Ottawa, and presided over by an elected Member of Parliament who assumed the position of Superintendent General. The lowest positions in the Indian Affairs bureaucracy were those of the Indian Agents, who were assigned to rural areas where they were to have direct contact with the Indian nations within their specific administrative region. The Indian Agent, as the local representative of the Department of Indian Affairs, was responsible for enforcing the strict measures of control outlined in the Indian Act, for administering assistance and medical aid where needed, and for promoting the assimilation program.

The Indian Act gave government agents extensive powers to control and intervene in the operation of reserve communities. In an effort to dismantle traditional forms of band government, the 1880 Indian Act gave government officials the authority to impose a form of elected local band government in a reserve community. The federal government exercised the right to remove any chief or council from office that government deemed "unfit to hold office" for reasons of incompetence, immorality, or intemperance.[17] Department officials could arbitrarily determine the structure of the band council and who could vote in its election. Elected band councils could make minor by-laws only subject to the Superintendent General's approval.

The Indian Act defined who could legally be considered an Indian. Officials encouraged the enfranchisement of Indians, a process through which they voluntarily gave up their Indian status and agreed to take up European economic practices, dress, and values. The enfranchisement program, quite literally, was devised for the purpose of eradicating Indians from Canadian society. Once an Indian had proven his willingness and ability to assume full citizenship, and that he was "of good moral character, temperate in his or her habits, and of sufficient intelligence to be qualified to hold land in fee simple," he could assume clear title to a tract of land from the reserve's holdings.[18] In encouraging the division of reserve lands into individual lots, federal officials sought to undermine the older system of collective ownership to one of individual property rights.[19] At times, notably between 1920-22, and 1932-60, the Indian Act gave the Department of Indian Affairs the power to enfranchise any Indian, with or without his consent.[20] The involuntary enfranchisement clause, on at least one occasion, was used by Department officials in an attempt to discredit influential Native leaders who were critical of the government.[21]

Coercive legislation aimed at assimilating Indians was not limited to political or economic domains. Amendments to the Indian Act in later years made it illegal for Native people to engage in their traditional cultural practices. The Indian Act in 1884 prohibited potlatches and any other ceremonies in which the giving away of goods occurred. The potlatch law was introduced in large part due to the lobbying of Christian missionaries in British Columbia, who realized the potlatch was a central cultural and political institution in Northwest Coast societies, and thus stood as a barrier to the establishment of missionary authority.[22] Furthermore, the massive giving away of goods was perceived to be in direct opposition to the value Europeans placed on the acquisition of private property. Later the Indian Act was amended to prohibit the Plains sun dances, and even to make it illegal for an Indian to participate in a parade or public ceremony in traditional dress without prior government approval.[23]

INDIAN EDUCATION

It was in the area of Indian education that missionaries and government agents collaborated most extensively. Prior to

Confederation, a number of day schools for Indians had been established by church denominations across Canada. The success of day schools, however, depended on the regular attendance of Indian children. While some Indian communities in Canada were relatively sedentary, the majority of Native peoples followed a lifestyle based on extensive seasonal movement between hunting, fishing, and trapping grounds. As one Superintendent General of Indian Affairs noted, "The progress of Indian children at day schools . . . is very greatly hampered and injuriously affected by the associations of their home life, and by the frequency of their absence, and the indifference of their parents to the regular attendance of their children at such schools."[24] By the late 1870s it was apparent to the federal government that the day school system was not meeting with the success that the church and state had hoped.

The residential school system, where children would be removed from their families and communities for months at a time, was created to resolve these problems. In 1879 the federal government commissioned Nicholas Davin to undertake a study of American Indian schools to determine the feasibility of adopting residential education in Canada. Indian residential schools in the United States were a key part of President Ulysses Grant's 1869 policy of "aggressive civilization," which envisioned the consolidation of Indian tribes onto reserves, the abolishment of tribal society and traditions, and the permanent settlement of individuals in their own homes and on their own tracts of land. A decade later officials reported that this policy was achieving "excellent" results.[25]

Residential schools in the United States were operated in two ways, either under the authority and direction of the Indian Affairs department, or under contract with various church denominations, which were given per capita grants for students. Students were provided with a basic academic training as well as instruction in agricultural, trade, and domestic skills. Against the recommendations of a prominent U.S. Indian Affairs official, who did not support the contract system because "the children at schools under contract do not, as a rule, get sufficient quantity of food," Davin went ahead and recommended that Indian residential schools in Canada be operated jointly by church and government.[26] Since many denominational schools already were in existence, a collaboration between the church and the state would not only be cost effective, but would enable the government to take advantage of the zeal and commitment of missionaries to bring about the "civilization" of Indians. So convinced was Davin of the importance of the civilizing program that he considered the establishment of schools not only a matter of policy, but a "sacred duty."[27] He suggested that four residential schools, providing an industrial education, be established immediately in the prairie region.

By 1880 the Canadian government had shifted its emphasis from the creation of day schools to the creation of residential schools. With this shift to residential schooling, the relationship between church and state now took a more formal cast: Indian education officially became a joint venture of church and state. While the federal government provided financial assistance and the legislative and bureaucratic apparatus for the establishment of Indian schools, various church denominations, mainly Roman Catholic, Anglican, Presbyterian, and Methodist, eagerly took on the responsibility for the management and day-to-day operation of the schools.[28] This arrangement suited both. By essentially subcontracting the responsibility for Indian education to the church denominations the federal government could save a significant amount of money. Further, the incorporation of a religious component in the curriculum was seen as a critical and necessary part of the assimilation process. For their part, the missionaries took advantage of the apparatus of the state to advance their own form of religious colonization. They acquired a literally captive audience to educate and convert to their particular faith without competition from other religious denominations.

Residential schools were of two types: boarding and industrial.[29] The former was geared to students up to fourteen years of age, and the school typically was situated on a reserve where it could draw a large number of Native children from the surrounding region. Industrial schools, on the other hand, usually were situated a long distance from Native villages and close to white population centers. The industrial schools were considered by the Department to be advanced schools where, in addition to basic reading and writing skills, children could be trained in such skills as industrial trades, agricultural, and domestic labour. The segregation of the students from their families and their cultural environment through industrial schools was seen by the Superintendent General of Indian Affairs to have two advantages: "[It] dissociates the Indian child from the deleterious home influences to which he would otherwise be subjected. It reclaims him from the uncivilized state in which he has been brought up."[30]

By 1894 the federal government was funding forty-five residential schools in Canada, eleven of which were in British Columbia.[31] Indian Affairs officials reported a marked increase in attendance at residential schools, which they interpreted as a sign of Indian parents' recognition of the positive aspects of the system. Anticipating that this support would be short-lived, however, government officials in this year took advantage of the lull in Native resistance to quietly pass an amendment to the Indian Act empowering Indian Agents to remove any school-age Indian child from his home to fill the residential schools. Nevertheless, by 1899, DIA officials were reporting that "the strong disinclination on the part of parents to the separation involved in letting [the students] go to industrial schools . . . remains more or less widespread."[32] The federal government continued to be optimistic about the success of the system, which was held up as a solution to the "Indian problem":

> If it were possible to gather in all the Indian children and retain them for a certain period, there would be produced a generation of English-speaking Indians, accustomed to the ways of civilized life, which might then be the dominant body among themselves, capable of holding its own with its white neighbours; and thus would be brought about a rapidly decreasing expenditure until the same should forever cease, and the Indian problem would have been solved.[33]

By the turn of the century, federal government expenditures on Indian education had risen exponentially from $18,000 in 1880 to over $300,000 in 1896.[34] The rising costs of funding industrial schools, coupled by poor attendance, unsatisfactory educational advancement, and concerns over the health of the students caused the federal government to place a moratorium on the construction of new industrial schools.[35] Nevertheless, the existing industrial schools continued to operate, despite mounting evidence that many of the buildings were old, dilapidated, and hazardous, and that in a number of schools the death rate of children was extremely high. For example, a 1907 report of P.H. Bryce, the Chief Medical Officer attached to the Department of Indian Affairs, found that in fifteen prairie residential schools, twenty-four percent of ex-students had died. At the File Hills school, which had been running for eighteen years, an alarming sixty-nine percent of ex-students had died of tuberculosis, contracted, the inspector believed, from the poor ventilation in the school's old and dilapidated buildings.[36] Bryce's report, which included detailed recommendations for alleviating the health problems at the schools, was ignored by the Department on the grounds that the proposed changes would be too costly.[37]

Despite such problems, residential schools continued to operate through the first half of the 1900s. By 1923 there were seventy-two residential schools in Canada, sixteen of which were in British Columbia.[38] Nine of these, situated at Williams Lake, Kamloops, Cranbrook, Fraser Lake, Sechelt, Squamish, Mission, Kuper Island, and Meares Island, were operated by the Roman Catholic church. Two, at Kitimat and Sardis, were run by the Methodists. The Anglican church ran three schools, one at Lytton and two at Alert Bay, while the Presbyterian church ran schools at Alberni and Ahousat on the west coast of Vancouver Island. The number of residential schools in Canada and in British Columbia remained fairly constant until the decline of the residential school system in the 1950s.

Through the first half of the century Indian education continued to consist of a mixture of academic, industrial, and moral training. The half day of academic instruction and half day of industrial training that Indian children were receiving in residential schools contrasted sharply with the increased emphasis on academic instruction offered to children in public schools.[39] The continued emphasis on vocational training for Indians was in part due to DIA officials' realization that the assimilation program was not succeeding; Native students leaving the residential schools were not becoming integrated into the dominant society. Consequently, federal officials supported a curriculum designed to provide Indians with only basic reading and writing skills and with training in such practical trades—animal husbandry, farming, blacksmithing, carpentry, and domestic skills—as might be useful to students when they returned to reserve life.[40]

In the decades after the Second World War, under increasing pressure from Canadian Indian leaders and with rising public concern for issues of poverty, civil rights, and racial equality, the federal government began steps to reform the administration of Indian affairs in Canada. Along with a major revision to the Indian Act in 1951, the federal government moved to phase out the residential school system and to encourage the establishment of day schools on reserves and integrated schooling in the public school system. By the 1980s the last remaining residential schools had closed.

THE RE-EMERGENCE OF THE RESIDENTIAL SCHOOL ISSUE

For much of the last century, Indian residential schools operated largely out of sight and mind of the Euro-Canadian public. In the late 1980s, media attention was sharply drawn to the Indian residential school system when a number of charges of sexual abuse of Native children were laid against members of the Roman Catholic and Anglican churches. These charges stemmed from incidents in church-run residential schools in British Columbia where the accused men had served as principals and supervisors. The consequences of the residential school system, however, go beyond the aftermath of individual instances of sexual abuse.

The impact of the residential school system has become the subject of much discussion both in First Nations communities and among the non-Native public in Canada. Native people across Canada are now speaking openly and publicly about their residential school experiences, and the suffering they underwent as a result of being separated from their families, being subjected to harsh physical punishment, being denied the right to speak their languages, and being indoctrinated with messages of personal and cultural inferiority. Many Native people are exploring the long-term psychological and social consequences of the residential school's assimilation program on First Nations communities. The consequences they have identified include high rates of alcoholism, suicide, and sexual abuse, the loss of language and culture, low self-esteem and pride, the breakdown of families, the loss of parenting skills, dependency on others, and loss of initiative.[41] For many Native people the residential school experience not only serves to explain many of the difficulties they have faced in their personal lives since leaving the schools, but also epitomizes on a small scale the deep-seated historical problems that have permeated Indian-white relations in Canada for centuries. So powerful is the residential school experience in current thought that it has been the most common issue raised by Native peoples across Canada in their presentations to the Royal Commission on Aboriginal Peoples.[42]

There is by no means a consensus about the nature and extent of the impact of the schools. In July 1991 the Oblates of Mary Immaculate, an order of the Roman Catholic church that operated most of the residential schools in Canada, issued a formal apology to Native people for the damage that the residential schools inflicted on Native communities.[43] Nevertheless, this apology sparked vigorous internal debate among the Oblates, and many church officials continue to defend the residential school system. They claim that many past students have positive memories of their time at the residential schools, that many parents willingly sent their children to the schools, and that isolated instances of sexual abuse do not detract from the overall good that the schools accomplished.[44] Some historians, too, have supported these claims. They argue that the residential schools had positive consequences—that the schools stimulated cultural resistance, fostered a pan-Indian identity and culture, and laid the groundwork for much of contemporary Indian rights movements[45]—and that students and parents exercised a significant amount of control over their children's attendance, and over the operation of the schools.[46]

These studies, by pointing out instances in which Native students complied or successfully resisted the system, fail to consider the role of coercion in shaping Native responses to the schools.[47] In celebrating resistance, the implicit message that 'the schools weren't that bad' not only serves as an apology for a deliberately destructive policy, but also draws attention away from the more important issue of the general structure of Indian-government relations. Left unexamined is the broader issue of how relations of unequal power between Native people, the church, and the government imposed limits not only on the possible avenues for resistance, but on how successful those forms of resistance could be. Because of the power structure within the residential schools, resistance usually took the form of subtle, indirect, and largely symbolic acts such as stealing food, lying, refusing to cry when punished, and speaking Native languages in private.[48] Efforts to bring about substantial changes in the operation of the residential schools were much less frequent and often unsuccessful.

In this book I take a closer look at the conditions that enabled challenges to the residential school system to arise, and the mechanisms that eventually thwarted these challenges. In order to do so it is necessary to turn again to an examination of the structural relationship between Native people and the Canadian government, and the beliefs about Indians that served to legitimize this relationship.

As previously discussed, the intent of Canadian Indian policy historically has been to assimilate Native people into the dominant society. Paradoxically, federal Indian policy in a number of ways has had the opposite effect. In order to justify and perpetuate its system of Indian administration, the Canadian government has identified Native peoples as a group who are somehow different, and who are presumed to need the paternalistic guidance of the dominant society in order to survive. The effect of the reserve system has been the geographical, social, and political segregation of Native peoples from the rest of Canadian society. A separate body of laws and a separate bureaucracy were created over a century ago to control and manage Indian peoples and to enforce the assimilative program. The effect of these legal and administrative structures, which are still in existence, has been: 1) the perpetuation of a separate Native identity; 2) the reinforcement of assumptions among both the government and the Euro-Canadian public that Native people are inherently incapable of directing their own lives; 3) the legitimization of a paternalistic system of government control that presumes to make decisions that are in the Native peoples' best interests; and 4) the enforcement of Native dependency on outside "helping" agencies ranging from government agents to missionaries to consultants.[49]

Native people have responded to the forces of change brought in through colonialism with both resistance and accommodation. It is not surprising, therefore, that First Nations people today have different understandings of their residential school experiences. Some students strenuously resisted the system, others quietly made the best of their circumstances, while still others became dedicated members of the church.

It is only when Native people begin to resist others' attempts to direct their lives that the dark side of the presumption of paternalism becomes apparent. Time after time, when Native people have resisted church and government interference, their resistance has been interpreted by officials only as confirmation of Native peoples' presumed inability to know what is best for them. In turn, this has served as evidence for the need for continued intervention. This ability of the church and government to redefine and absorb acts of resistance is an important mechanism that creates the impression that Native people will continue to require church and government guidance in perpetuity.[50]

For this reason direct resistance to the residential school system tended to have the opposite effect: it reinforced the racist belief that Native people were inherently 'wild' and resistant to discipline, and that the residential school system was a necessary and important component of the 'civilizing' program. The church and government maintained their control over Native people not only through legal and bureaucratic power, but by being able to control the meaning of events and protests. These three types of control—legal, administrative, and ideological—are all evident in this case study of the Williams Lake residential school.

By looking at the impact of the residential school system in the broader context of the structural relationship between Native peoples and the federal government, a larger problem becomes apparent. This larger problem is not that the Indian residential school system existed, or that its effects may have been good or bad, but that certain groups in society have presumed to know what is in Native peoples' best interests, and that these groups have held, and continue to hold, the power and authority to interfere in Native people's lives and to enforce conditions that Native people oppose.

In the following pages a brief ethnographic sketch of the northern Shuswap and their early response to European settlers, government agents, and missionaries is presented. I then focus on a series of events that took place during the first three decades of operation of the Williams Lake residential school. At various times during this period complaints were made by the parents of students, by local white settlers, and by Department of Indian Affairs officials themselves, about the treatment of students at the school and about the activities of the Oblate priests. The Department of Indian Affairs conducted three separate investigations, in 1899, 1902, and 1920, into allegations of mistreatment of students at the school. A close look at these events reveals the complex relationships that existed between the Department of Indian Affairs, the Oblate missionaries, and the Native communities. Each party involved in the controversy had its own motives for raising concerns or responding to charges, and each had its own interests to protect. In the end, the concerns of the children and their families were dismissed, only to be used as fuel to legitimize the civilizing mandate of the residential school system and federal Indian policy in general. The events described in the following pages occurred in the early years of the school's operation. Nevertheless, some of the key factors that prevented problems at the school from being resolved continue to exist today despite the closing of the Williams Lake residential school in 1981.

CHAPTER TWO

The Shuswap Response to Colonialism

DUNCAN STICKS AND AUGUSTINE ALLAN were born into a world that had undergone dramatic change over the last century. In the early 1800s the northern Shuswap of the central interior of British Columbia followed a semi-nomadic hunting and gathering lifestyle that had remained relatively stable for generations.[1] In the summer groups of families gathered on the banks of the Fraser River to harvest the annual salmon runs, which provided the bulk of food for the fall and winter months. In the fall families dispersed through the mountain regions to the southwest and northeast of the Fraser River to hunt for deer, elk, and caribou, which were also important sources of food. Families congregated during the winter months in semi-permanent villages situated along the Fraser River and along small creeks feeding into this river. In the spring, the food supplies almost spent, families moved out of their villages and spread out to dig roots and to fish for trout on distant lakes, gathering once again at the Fraser River in the summer to fish for salmon.

Shuswap bands consisted of groups of related families that wintered together in the same general area. Each band, which was named after the territory it occupied, had one principal winter village with several smaller family settlements a distance removed. Northern Shuswap bands had, on average, about 200 members loosely related to each other through either the mother's or the father's line. At the center of each band was a core group of relatives, related through the father's line, who lived closely together and who exercised control over the land and its resources. The hereditary chief, who was a member of this core group, was responsible for regulating, if necessary, the use of salmon fishing stations, berry patches, and root digging grounds, and for ensuring that all families within the band got an equal share of these resources.

As a rule marriages were not permitted between close blood relatives, including second cousins. After marriage the wife usually would move to the household of her husband. As a result of these marriage practices a network of relatives existed that connected all of the Shuswap bands in the region. Visiting relatives in distant bands was a common activity, with individuals and families often staying with distant relatives during the winter months. Kinship networks also extended into the bands of neighbouring Carrier, Chilcotin, and Lillooet nations, with whom the northern Shuswap had frequent contact. Having relatives in distant bands was an important strategy for survival. During times when foods became scarce in one region relatives in other regions could be called upon to provide food and to share their hunting, fishing, and gathering territories. Kinship ties, language, and shared cultural values and beliefs were key mechanisms that integrated the Shuswap people of the Cariboo region.

Shuswap life began to change, with increasing momentum, in the 1800s. The first white person to enter northern Shuswap country was Simon Fraser, who arrived in 1808 on his exploration of the river that now bears his name. Trading posts were built at Fort Kamloops in 1812 and Fort Alexandria in 1821, and in the following decades a busy fur trade existed between the Shuswap and the Europeans. The fur trade resulted in some changes to the seasonal cycles and economic activities of the Shuswap. More time was spent in trapping, and in exchange the Shuswap acquired new technology: firearms, steel traps, knives, kettles, and blankets. Nevertheless, the fur trade is best characterized as a reciprocal relationship from which both the Shuswap and the European traders benefitted.[2] Since the traders relied on the Shuswap to remain in their territories for trapping to continue, and since trapping could be incorporated without too much disruption to the seasonal subsistence activities, Shuswap control over their land and resources was not seriously threatened.

Two events in the 1860s dramatically changed Shuswap life. The first was the discovery by whites of gold in Shuswap territory. Between 1858 and 1864 thousands of white and Asian miners flooded into the Cariboo in what became known as the Cariboo Gold Rush. The miners travelled up the Fraser River by way of old aboriginal trails that connected villages, fishing camps, and hunting and gathering grounds. The completion in 1863 of a major highway from the Lower Mainland to the Cariboo gold fields meant even more non-Natives entering Shuswap lands. The miners fanned out on the major river systems of the Cariboo, in the process displacing many Shuswap families from their hunting, trapping, and fishing grounds.

The Shuswap's customary means of defending their territorial boundaries and responding to trespass was to launch defensive and retaliatory war raids. Yet by the 1860s the weight and power of white laws was beginning to be felt. In 1864, in an incident that became known as the Chilcotin war, some Chilcotin men murdered a crew of white men who were building a road into Chilcotin territory.[3] Six Chilcotin men subsequently were arrested, taken to Quesnel, and tried for murder. Five of the men were convicted and hanged with much publicity and ceremony. The Chilcotin had responded to the trespass on their land in a culturally appropriate manner. The new government, however, was determined to demonstrate its authority in the new colony. By prosecuting the Chilcotin men the government sought to reassure the white public, and to send a signal to the Native people, that Native resistance to the expansion of the colonial frontier would be dealt with severely.

The second event was the smallpox epidemic of 1862-63. The epidemic, which swept across the Chilcotin plateau into Shuswap territory, completely wiped out the six Shuswap bands on the west side of the Fraser River and cut the overall Shuswap population to a third of its former level.[4] A white settler at Williams Lake wrote to a friend in February, 1863, and described the scene:

> I have not yet taken the small pox and I think there is no danger now. The Indians have got over it now all around. There was 12 of them died here. They were camped right over at the Creek where you used to get the water sometimes, when the stream would be dry. There was 15 of them & only 3 of them lived & at Beaver Lake out of fifty-one only three survived.[5]

Duncan Sticks' father Johnny was a survivor of the 1862-63 smallpox epidemic. Johnny was a child of seven when the disease swept through the families of the Alkali Lake band.

Their social networks shattered, the survivors were forced to reorganize themselves, form new family units, and continue living as best they could. As the gold rush ended, many miners stayed in the area and began to clear land, put up fences, and establish ranches and farms. As a result it became more and more difficult for the Shuswap to live on hunting and fishing alone. Shuswap families began to cultivate crops, especially potatoes, as an additional food source. Some Shuswap men took on jobs as packers and guides along the gold field routes, and were drawn into the rough, alcohol-soaked culture of white frontier life.

The waves of legislative and administrative colonialism continued. In 1881 an Indian Agency was established in the region of Williams Lake, and the local Indian Agent immediately began efforts to impose the terms and conditions of the Indian Act on the nearby Shuswap communities. By this decade conflicts between Natives and settlers over lands had reached a height, fuelled by the failure of both the previous colonial government, and now the current provincial government, to recognize aboriginal title and sign treaties with the Native nations of the province. As settlement expanded the Shuswap found it difficult to protect even their village sites and cultivated fields from pre-emption. During the 1860s the colonial government had responded to the increasing land conflicts between the Shuswap and white settlers by setting aside reserves for the northern Shuswap bands of Soda Creek, Canoe Creek, and Alkali Lake. Nevertheless, by 1871 these reserves had been officially erased from the government record. In the meantime, the 1870 Land Act prohibited Indians from pre-empting land, while white settlers could apply for free grants of up to 320 acres. As a result, the Shuswap had no legal recourse to protect their lands.

Much of the best agricultural land was taken up by whites, while the Shuswap were gradually pushed onto marginal, dry regions where agriculture was difficult. In 1879, after the failure of that year's salmon runs, the situation of the Williams Lake Shuswap was desperate. Chief William spoke eloquently of his peoples' dilemma:

> I am an Indian Chief and my people are threatened by starvation. The white men have taken all the land and all the fish. A vast country was ours. It is all gone. The noise of the threshing machine and the wagon has frightened the deer and the beaver. We have nothing to eat. My people are sick. My young men are angry. All the Indians from Canoe Creek to the headwaters of the Fraser say: 'William is an old woman. He sleeps and starves in silence.' I am old and feeble and my authority diminishes every day. I am sorely puzzled. I do not know what I say next week when the chiefs are assembled in a council. A war with the white man will end in our destruction, but death in war is not so bad as death by starvation.[6]

In the end, under the influence of peacemakers like Chief William, the Shuswap did not resort to violence to protect their lands. Instead, in order to survive, the Shuswap were forced to acquiesce in a number of ways to the powers of the expanding Canadian state. The bands accepted the small reserves that were finally established for them in the early 1880s. The Shuswap adopted European clothing, technology, and foods. They became part-time farmers and took occasional jobs as labourers on ranches and farms. Many became bi- or multi-lingual, speaking French, English, and the Chinook trade jargon in addition to their first language, Shuswap. Major rifts had appeared within the Shuswap communites between those promoting conciliation with whites and those promoting violence. The authority of the Shuswap chiefs was seriously threatened and they struggled to keep their communities together.

Yet, despite the establishment of reserves, the Shuswap continued to live a semi-mobile lifestyle, moving between hunting grounds, fishing camps, and the reserve villages. They still gathered together at feasts to socialize, gamble, and perform songs and dances, and shamans continued to hold a prominent position in the communities and to help the sick. Despite the divisive strains, their shared kinship ties, language, and cultural values reinforced a sense of common identity among the Shuswap of the Cariboo.

It was the next wave of colonialism, arriving with the Roman Catholic missionaries, that interfered most profoundly with the cultural and moral dimensions of Shuswap life.

MISSIONARIES IN THE CARIBOO: THE EARLY YEARS

In 1838 the Roman Catholic missionary Modeste Demers, established a mission in Oregon territory, which became the first Catholic mission west of the Rocky Mountains and north of California.[7] In 1842 Demers undertook a reconnaissance survey of the central interior of British Columbia to test Native receptivity to the Catholic church. Demers reported that he was well received by the Shuswap and Carrier people he visited.[8] John Nobli, a Jesuit priest, visited the area between 1845 and 1847, staying at Fort Alexandria and paying visits to the nearby villages. Nevertheless, missionary activity was sporadic until 1867, when the Oblates of Mary Immaculate, a

French order of the Roman Catholic Church, established a mission in the heart of Shuswap country. St. Joseph's Mission, situated in the San Jose valley several kilometers south of Williams Lake, signalled the beginning of a permanent missionary presence in the area.

From the outset the Oblates determined that the Mission would be self-supporting, and the site was carefully chosen to include some of the most fertile agricultural lands in the district.[9] In the following years the Mission established a successful farm and ranch operation, providing not only for the needs of the resident Oblates but also turning a profit through the sale of cattle, horses, and farm products on the local market.

The Oblates' system for evangelizing the Native populations began with the establishment of a central mission, from where missionaries would make regular tours to the surrounding Native villages. Where possible, the Oblates sought to preach in Native languages, use Native catechists, and blend elements of the Catholic faith with indigenous beliefs.[10] At the same time, Native practices that the Oblates perceived would hinder their long-term goals, or that were inimical to Catholic beliefs and morality, were vigorously criticized. One of the Oblates' primary goals was to establish themselves as intermediaries between Natives and colonial society, from which position the missionaries could protect Native people from the vices—drunkenness and prostitution—that were believed to be an inevitable consequence of contact with non-Native society. From this position the Oblates also could exercise their authority and implement their program for civilizing the Native population without the interference of government officials.

The Oblates thus began their campaign to convert the Shuswap, Carrier, and Chilcotin people from their own values and beliefs to that of the Catholic faith. The missionaries launched an intense moral battle against the Native practices of feasting, dancing, gambling, and shamanism. The Oblates defined their relationship with respect to Native people as that of paternalistic protectors, and they sincerely believed that conversion to Catholicism and the "civilized" ways of a settled agrarian life was in the Native people's best interests. Although the missionaries sought to change Native culture, at times, especially in the few decades after the 1860s, they acted also as advocates for Native people, providing food and help to Shuswap communities left landless due to white settlement, and lobbying the government for a quick settlement of the Indian land issue.[11]

Were it not for other factors, the missionaries' attempts to dismantle Native culture and convert Native people to Catholicism would have had little impact. However, the missionaries followed on the heels of the gold rush, the small-pox epidemic, and the gradual loss of Shuswap control over their lands and lives. The increasing moral authority that the missionaries wielded over Native people was part of a more general process of domination of Native societies by colonial forces.

THE WILLIAMS LAKE
RESIDENTIAL SCHOOL

The Oblates were encouraged by the initial responses to their missionary activity in the Cariboo. By 1880 churches had been built in almost all of the Native villages in the area, and hundreds of children and adults had been baptized. However, churches and baptisms were only superficial symbols of conversion. The Oblates realized that their efforts were being hampered by the semi-nomadic lifestyle that the Shuswap continued to follow. Despite missionary visits, the Shuswap were continuing to practice many of their cultural traditions. As a result, the Oblates of St. Joseph's Mission began to apply more and more pressure on the federal government to fund a school for the Native children of the Cariboo. Father McGuckin of St. Joseph's Mission, writing in 1878, believed that a residential school would be the only answer to the missionaries' problems:

> In a few years hence all our young boys and girls will speak English, mix with the whites and lose all of their original simplicity. To resist them the temptations that will be placed in their way nothing less than a thorough religious education will suffice. This they will never acquire in their own language. Not as children, for during childhood there is no opportunity so long as they remain with their parents. Not during boyhood or girlhood, for then they are too busy and can only be found for a short time in the winter, and often then unwilling to occupy their spare time at religious instruction. Hence if we will preserve the faith amongst them, and provide them with arms to resist temptation, we must endeavor to get them into school and keep them for a certain number of years.[12]

Earlier attempts to operate schools for both Native and white children in the area had been foiled by inadequate financing, problems securing teaching staff, and competition from other schools in the region.[13] Finally, in 1891 the

Oblates and the federal government reached an agreement on the creation of an industrial school for Indian children. The Williams Lake industrial school, also known as St. Joseph's residential school, the Williams Lake residential school, or, locally, as 'the Mission,' opened its doors in 1891. The school was to have a profound impact on the lives of three generations of Native people in the Cariboo-Chilcotin region.

CHAPTER THREE

The Early Years
of the Mission School

EDUCATION AND DISCIPLINE

THE PHILOSOPHY OF CHILD-REARING and education that was enacted at St. Joseph's Mission contrasted sharply with that practiced among the
Shuswap, Carrier, and Chilcotin peoples. In northern hunting and gathering societies knowledge was not acquired pas-
sively from formal, external sources. Instead, children learned
the skills they needed to survive, and the beliefs, values, and
codes of behaviour appropriate to their society, by a trial-and-
error process of observing and imitating adult behaviour and
by listening to stories in which ethical concepts and morals
were imbedded. These indirect, non-authoritarian educational techniques fostered in children a sense of individual
autonomy and self-confidence. Consequently, the children
who entered the Williams Lake residential school came from
cultures which placed great emphasis on direct experience as
the best form of education.[1]

The system of childrearing and education practiced at the
residential school was different. Knowledge was to be gained
not by heeding one's own ideas and intuition, but by accepting
without question the truths presented by external authorities.

Strict discipline, regimented behaviour, submission to authority, and corporal punishment were central characteristics of the Oblates' educational philosophy. This system of education was a natural product of both the Roman Catholic church's hierarchical institutional structure and world view, and its ecclesiastic system of penances for breaching rigid codes of moral conduct. In fact, since the 1600s Roman Catholic missionaries had been imposing systems of strict discipline on their Native converts, and punishing Native transgressors with public humiliations and floggings.[2]

Further, the Oblates' system of education was fully compatible with 19th-century British educational philosophy, and thus was not regarded as unusual by British colonial administrators in Canada. By the nineteenth century the belief that corporal punishment was good for the child, and that breaking the child's will was a critical part of child rearing, were generally-accepted beliefs among the Christian Euro-Canadian public, regardless of their denomination.[3] From this cultural perspective, Indian children were seen as lacking discipline. "Indian parents are too easy on their children . . . Indians have a holy horror of anything that smacks [of] system and order," one Roman Catholic Bishop commented.[4] Discipline and the submission to external authority were the first lessons to which the children were subjected at the Williams Lake residential school.

The Oblate missionaries at Williams Lake were fully aware of the difficulties that lay ahead of them. They realized that for the school to be successful not only must incoming students submit to a foreign educational system based on strict obedience to hierarchical authority, but that these students too, as time wore on, had to serve as role models to facilitate the submission of new students entering the school.

Consequently, the size of the first group of students to be enrolled in the Mission was limited to twelve:

> It will be easier and more expeditious in the long run to have a number that you can thoroughly attend to and particularly instruct as to a knowledge of the English language and discipline than to have so many, considering that they are taken from their native wilds and have been accustomed to no control whatever, that it would be impossible to give them what individual attention required at the commencement. After the first batch of boys learn something of English and have become amenable to the rules and regulations governing their conduct and daily action at school, then half the trouble is removed as each of these partially trained lads will really occupy the position of an instructor by example and communication. The institution is to have the full number of boys within the year.[5]

Enrollment at the school gradually increased through the 1890s. By 1896-97, fifty students were officially enrolled. In 1915-16, this had increased to sixty-four, and by 1932 the enrollment had reached 120.[6]

LIFE AT THE SCHOOL

According to the terms of the original agreement with the federal government, the Oblates committed themselves to provide the children with board, clothing, care, education, and training in two or three trades, which in the early years were carpentry, harness-making, and blacksmithing. Agricultural skills also were an important part of industrial training.

The girls were taught housekeeping, butter making, sewing, knitting, "and such accomplishments in that line as are deemed most essential in fitting them for the life before them."[7] The students received a half day in academic studies and a half day in industrial or domestic skills.

The school was run by an Oblate principal. In the early years the girls were taught both academic and domestic skills by nuns of the Sisters of St. Ann, and after 1896 by the Sisters of the Child Jesus. The boys initially were taught academics and trade skills by lay people; however, in 1902 both religious and laymen were employed as trade and agricultural instructors, while the Sisters of the Child Jesus took over the academic training of the boys.[8] The boys and girls were housed in separate buildings, which also contained classrooms. The Oblate priests resided in the boys' building, the Sisters in the girls' building.

The physical isolation of children from their families and communities was a central ingredient of the residential school system. Toward the end of the second school year, however, parents began protesting to the local Indian Agent of the Williams Lake District that they wished to have their children released for a month during the summer to allow them to spend time with their families. Indian Agent Meason supported the idea and brought the issue to the attention of Father Lejacq, principal of the school. However, Lejacq was concerned with the financial implications. Writing to the Federal Indian Superintendent of British Columbia, A.W. Vowell, Lejacq stated that:

> If the government wants to give vacation to the children, it is all
> right, but as the government has been paying according to the

number of days of attendance, in order to get the whole grant I am entitled to, I will have to count, in the report, the vacation days as full days.[9]

Officials in the Department of Indian Affairs refused the request. The Deputy Superintendent General in Ottawa insisted that the per capita fee of $130 was to reflect the number of days the students were actually in residence. He refused to permit "paid leave" for the students.[10] Lejacq, on his end, was unwilling to compromise the scant funding the Oblates received for operating the school. The wishes of the students and their parents were therefore overridden by the financial concerns of the Department and the Oblate Mission.

That autumn a new Indian Agent took over from Meason. Indian Agent Johns assured Vowell that "the Principal J.M.J. Lejacq simply wishes to return to the old order of things; I quite agree with him that a continuous attendance will be better for the pupils."[11] Although the decision had been made on financial grounds, it now was legitimized as being in the students' best interests.

COMPLAINTS FROM
LOCAL BUSINESSMEN

The financial problems that the residential school was facing were caused in part by the Department of Indian Affairs' failure to live up to its original agreement with the Oblates. According to this agreement, the Department of Indian Affairs was to fund the residential school on the basis of fifty pupils. However, in 1892-93, and again in 1893-94, the per capita grant was arbitrarily reduced to twenty-five students.

THE EARLY YEARS OF THE MISSION SCHOOL

The Oblates were having difficulty getting the balance owed to them by the Department, and as a result the school was heavily in debt. The sale of agricultural products and goods manufactured by students became a vital source of income for the Mission.

By the turn of the century the non-Native population of Williams Lake region consisted of widely dispersed farming and ranching homesteads. The principal center was 150 Mile House, located several kilometers southeast of the head of Williams Lake and close to St. Joseph's Mission. Both the name and the importance of 150 Mile House were due to its position on Cariboo Wagon Road and its distance from Mile 0 at Lillooet. A general store, telegraph office, hotel, and provincial police station were situated here. 150 Mile House was an important junction for the express routes. From here mail, freight, and passengers were transported by stagecoach northward to Horsefly and Quesnel, westward to the Chilcotin, and south to Alkali Lake.[12] The village of Williams Lake itself, at the foot of the lake, had been bypassed when the Cariboo Road had been built in 1863, and would not gain prominence for another two decades with the arrival of the Pacific Great Eastern railroad in 1919.

British, Irish, European, and American immigrants had been arriving in the Cariboo in a steady stream since the 1860s. Many had married Native women and established families, homes, and ranches. By 1901 the settler population in the vicinity of Williams Lake was about 350, a number which included about seventy Chinese immigrants and their families who were making a living by trapping, gold mining, and working as labourers on ranches and as cooks and waiters in hotels along the wagon road.[13] The Shuswap people in the Williams Lake region, despite having been devastated by diseases and loss of land, remained the majority of the area population at about 500.[14]

With the local economy based primarily on small-scale ranching, agriculture, mining, and transportation, the training in trades and agricultural skills offered by the Mission was seen as appropriate to the local context. However, though the Mission in earlier years had had the full moral and financial support of the local settlers, the Oblates' practice of selling goods and articles on the local market now was generating a significant amount of hostility from local businessmen.

In 1894 a Mr. E.C. Davison of the Kamloops Harness Emporium wrote a letter of complaint to his local Member of Parliament and to B.C. Indian Superintendent Vowell regarding the operation of the trades department at the Mission school. Davison accused the school of running a profit-making manufacturing business, and selling goods on the local market for low prices. As a result, Davison's store at Clinton was losing customers: "It is impossible for any person carrying on a legitimate business in these lines to compete with such an institution as this, as they can manufacture goods at penitentiary prices." He raised two questions: the purpose of the trades department, and whether the school was authorized by the Department of Indian Affairs to conduct such business.[15]

The Department of Indian Affairs realized that the school needed a supplementary income to support its operation. In a note to the Superintendent General, the Deputy Superintendent General stated:

> The amount contributed by the Government to these schools [those funded on the per capita basis] is not sufficient for their entire maintenance, and the Management must sell the product

of the industries taught in the institutions in order to provide sufficient revenue.[16]

Rather than accept financial responsibility for the situation and increase the level of Departmental funding to the school, Department officials chose to support the Oblates' business ventures. Lejacq refused to stop selling goods on the local market. Instead, he offered to sell Davison all of the goods manufactured at the school at a wholesale price, leaving him a margin for fair profit. A similar offer was made to two other local businesses. This did not quell the hostility of the local businessmen, and five years later another effort to discredit the Mission was launched.

MORE COMPLAINTS: 1899-1900

In the spring of 1899 an anonymous resident of the Williams Lake area sent a letter of complaint about the Mission to the Department of Indian Affairs in Ottawa. A series of charges were made: that the school was receiving funding on an illegitimate basis, as they admitted white and 'half-breed' children as a strategy for filling the attendance rolls and securing the full per capita payment; that the children were being poorly cared for and were receiving an inadequate education; and, most important, that the students were being used simply as cheap labourers to support a profitable business which then cut into the business of other local merchants.[17]

The tactic of writing directly to the Superintendent General, the highest position within the Department of Indian

Affairs, proved effective. B.C. Indian Superintendent A.W. Vowell was instructed to investigate the school.[18] Vowell and Indian Agent Bell from the Williams Lake Indian Agency paid what they described later as an "unexpected" visit to the school on May 2 and 3. An unannounced visit was necessary, Vowell thought, since "had the management of the school received due notice of the day and hour of my arrival the investigation contemplated could not be as satisfactory or thorough as was under the circumstances desirable."[19] In other words, Vowell feared that the Oblates would attempt to hide the true conditions of life at the school.

After spending two days inspecting the facilities and interviewing the students, both Agent Bell and Vowell concluded that all was fine at the school.[20] In his report, Vowell stated that he was

> . . . highly pleased with the children's attainments and the kind, efficient and painstaking qualities exhibited by the Instructor of the boys as well as the Revd. Sisters who have charge of the girls. The pupils looked well and happy, and deserved to have every confidence in and respect for, their teachers.[21]

Both Bell and Vowell supported the school's practice of selling goods on the local market. The goods were of excellent quality, they pointed out, and a certain amount of profit from sales was not unreasonable. Both suggested that the existence of local opposition to the school had been exaggerated, since "no one complains that there is a cut in prices to interfere with other parties," and since "residents and frequent travellers avail themselves of the facilities offered at the school for having repairs done."

The only complaint that Vowell had was the tattered and

ill-fitting clothing of the children. The management of the school agreed to improve this situation. Nevertheless, Vowell took additional steps to remind the Oblates of their accountability to the Department. On his return to Vancouver Vowell met with Bishop Durieu, who "assured me that whatever the Department most desired would be attended to."[22] In reporting this Vowell also was assuring his own superiors that the Department was taking seriously its responsibility to oversee the care of the Mission's students.

Local protests did not stop there. A year later E.A. Carew-Gibson, managing director of the Cariboo Trading Company and a resident of 150 Mile House, wrote a bitter letter to Superintendent Vowell. He complained that the Mission was continuing to undercut local traders by selling grain and hay below market value. He accused the Oblates of using their religion to secure cheap labour and government subsidization for what, in essence, was a business venture, and he demanded that the Department put an end to the Mission's involvement in local trading.[23]

Once again both the principal of the school, Father Peytavin, and Indian Agent Bell denied the accusations.[24] They insisted that regular prices were being charged for goods, and that the local settlers, who did not have Carew-Gibson's vested interests, supported this trade. The principal argued that the Department was getting a good deal for their money, and that if it were not for the Oblates' farm operation the school would not have the finances to continue operating. He expressed confidence in the Department's "impartial investigations" and hoped that their good relations with the Department would continue. The persistent attacks on the Mission, however, were beginning to wear on the Oblates.

Priests' and boys' residence, St. Joseph's Mission, ca 1900.   PHOTO: BRITISH COLUMBIA ARCHIVES AND RECORDS SERVICE

Students being taught knitting and needlework by Sisters of the Child Jesus, St. Joseph's Mission, ca 1900.

PHOTO: NATIONAL ARCHIVES OF CANADA

Class of 1903-4, St. Joseph's Mission. Mary Sticks, sister of Duncan, is second row from front, second from left. Sister Euphrasia is in the middle with young girl on her lap. Father Boening is in back row. The boy on left, second row from back, has had his head shaved, a common form of punishment for runaways. PHOTO: IRENE STRANGOE

Girls' class of 1908-9, St. Joseph's Mission. PHOTO: JOSEPHINE BOB

The garden at St. Joseph's Mission, summer of 1908. The Sisters of the Child Jesus are shown picking raspberries.

PHOTO: JOSEPHINE BOB

CHAPTER FOUR

A Death and an Inquest

T HE FREQUENCY OF CHILDREN running away from the Mission increased in 1901 and 1902. It was now obvious to officials within the Department of Indian Affairs that the Oblates were having trouble controlling the students and managing the operation of the school. Then, in February 1902, an incident occurred that brought the crisis in school management to a head. Nine boys ran away from the Mission one afternoon in early February. Eight of them were captured and returned, but one, a boy from Alkali Lake, was not discovered until the next day, when he was found dead. When word reached Ottawa of the student's death, the Department demanded an immediate investigation by Super-intendent Vowell into the circumstances of the boy's death and the general state of care being provided to the students at the Williams Lake residential school.

Under Vowell's direction, Indian Agent Bell visited the school in mid-February and interviewed the teachers, students, and the principal. Bell reported that of the nine boys that had run away, two had been from Alkali Lake, three from Williams Lake, and four from Canim Lake. The boys had begun to head for their respective villages, breaking into three separate groups. The teacher who had been supervising the boys in the field at the time of their escape had captured the three from Williams Lake. The two from Alkali Lake were then spotted at a distance. The teacher caught up to the first and demanded that he remain where he was while he continued on in pursuit of the other boy. While the other boy was caught, the first disappeared. Meanwhile, the principal and a school employee left in pursuit of the Canim Lake boys, who were eventually returned to the school. Eight-year-old Duncan Sticks, the boy who had disappeared, was the one found dead the next day, thirteen kilometers from the school.

Agent Bell had these remarks on this subject:

> I examined the boys as to their reason for running away from school and the only reason they gave me was 'The teacher whips us'. I asked them if it was the Principal they said no . . . asked if he whipped their head they said 'no' only on the legs. The teacher showed me his book where a record of all the chastisement the pupils get is kept and I must say they are slight indeed compared to the time I went to school. I asked the boys why they were whipped and the reply was 'When we don't have our lessons'. I have frequent letters from the parents of the boys who have been running away from this institution asking me to find out why the boys run off . . . claiming they cannot do so from their children. My own opinion is there is no good reason for their absconding only the wild nature of the Indian hates confinement as they are well fed and cared for.[1]

In short, Bell summarized the problem as being due to the 'wild nature' of Indians and due to the inability of the Oblates, shorthanded as they were, to constantly supervise the students. The problem, as Bell saw it, was lack of discipline.

Bishop Dontenwill of New Westminster also responded to Superintendent Vowell's concerns about the lax management of the Mission. He put forth arguments that were essentially the same as those offered by Agent Bell. According to Dontenwill, there were two components to the problem. First was the difficulty that the Oblates had in finding satisfactory teachers for the boys. The unreliability of the lay teachers had contributed to the lack of discipline. Second, the spirit of · rebellion had been spreading amongst the student population:

> The symptoms of a serious determination to leave school especially on the girl's [sic] part were deep set and it was evident for any one who was acquainted with the Indian character that they would try again. *Harsh measures were tried but to the only purpose of setting the Indians, as a whole, against the school* [emphasis added].[2]

Third, the Bishop firmly believed that the students' reasons for running away were "childish," and that the real reason was that the Indian students were unused to discipline. This, he argued, reflected a racial character of Indians:

> Indians have a holy horror of anything which smacks [of] system and order . . . [Indians have a] habitual and innate disposition to shirk what is so irksome to them. They do not realize the weakness in their character . . . when Indian children are brought face to face with the necessity of going against their hereditary inclinations to indulge in their love for independence and are restrained in their habits of disorder, it is not surprising that they should wish to throw off the yoke of discipline.[3]

Part of the blame lay with the parents, who were "too easy on their children, and they believe too willingly what their children tell them." A previous teacher had been equally guilty of encouraging the boys to run away:

> He did the boys harm by talking to them about the Father's want of love for the Indians etc. He also made the boys write to their parents to complain. This man was instrumental in putting an idea in some of the boys' heads that they were big enough and that they could earn money if they left the school, and that the school was keeping them to get work out of them.[4]

Having laid out, and confined, the roots of the problem, Dontenwill assured Vowell that he was willing to receive any suggestions the Department might offer as to how to improve the situation at the school.

If this situation had been effectively contained within Oblate and Department of Indian Affairs circles the matter might have been laid to rest. However, some non-Native residents of the Williams Lake area had got wind of the troubles. Carew-Gibson, a local businessman with a history of antagonism toward the Mission, and a Mr. Brophy, an ex-teacher at the school, began putting pressure on the Attorney General of the province to hold an inquest into the death of the boy.[5] Carew-Gibson undoubtedly saw this as an opportunity to attack the Oblates at the Mission who, in his view, had been unfairly cutting into his trading business for years. Brophy had been dismissed recently for being drunk and absent from the school. He may well have been motivated by personal vindictiveness, but he may also have been genuinely concerned for the welfare of the students.

Both men were implying that the Principal of the school was attempting to cover up the circumstances of the boy's death.[6]

Indian Agent Bell informed Vowell of these developments by private letter.[7] Bell warned that Brophy was "a smoothe [sic] and polished talker" who was claiming to have documented evidence of "everything happening at the school; food, whippings etc." Although Bell himself thought that an inquest was not warranted, he was worried, and he thought he should notify Vowell that trouble was brewing so that Vowell could prepare himself should the Attorney General want to interview him.

The fact remained that the body of the child had not been examined by a coroner before it had been buried. As a result, questions were still in the air regarding the cause of death. How had Duncan Sticks died? Why had no examination taken place? Was it a deliberate cover-up?

THE INQUEST

An inquest into the death of Duncan Sticks began on February 28 and lasted for five days. It alternated in location between Alkali Lake and 150 Mile House. The object of the inquest was to determine "when, where, how and after what manner" the boy, Duncan Sticks, had come to his death.[8] The local coroner and a six-man jury, comprising local non-Native residents, heard evidence from a wide range of sources. Eight students and ex-students gave statements about their experiences while at the school. Five Native men, among them several parents of students and the father of the dead boy, were interviewed and their statements were recorded.

66

The boys' teacher, the trades instructor, the Sister Superior of the girls' school, the principal Father Boening, and Father Chiappini of St. Joseph's Mission all gave sworn statements. Two local white men, one who had discovered the body, were also interviewed. The body, which had been buried at Alkali Lake three weeks earlier, was dug up and examined by Coroner Hoops, who then gave evidence as to the probable cause of death.

Why had the students run away?
The students gave consistent testimony of being forced to eat rotten food, being constantly hungry, and being whipped for not following orders. These conditions, the children said, were the reasons they had tried to run away from school.

Ellen Charlie, age 16:
"I ran away four times because the Sisters and Fathers did not treat me good; they gave us bad food which was fit only for pigs, the meat was rotten, and had a bad smell and taste . . . when I did not eat it they gave it to me again for the next meal. . . . They would sometimes lock me in a room and make me kneel down for half an hour or an hour. They once kept me locked up for a week. . . . They sometimes whipped me with a strap on the face and sometimes stripped me and whipped me."[9]

Christine Haines:
"I ran away twice from the school because the Sisters dident [sic] treat me good—they gave me rotten food to eat and punished me for not eating it—the meat and the soup were rotten and tasted so bad they made the girls sick sometimes . . . they shut me up in a room by myself for 3 days and gave me bread and water—the

room was cold and dark—they beat me with a strap, sometimes on the face, and sometimes took my clothes off and beat me. This is the reason I ran away."[10]

Mary Sticks, age 11:
"The sisters scold me all the time—they gave me bad food—the beef was rotten—I couldent [sic] eat it—they kept it over and gave it to me next meal—they tied my hands and blindfolded me and gave me nothing to eat for a day. . . . I was never allowed to speak to my brother [Duncan] at the school, and dont [sic] know how he was treated . . ."[11]

François, age 10:
Ran away from the school once about the 8th of February when the other boys ran away—he ran awy [sic] because the teacher beat him too much—he was beaten on the legs with a strap, but was never cut, was also beaten on the hands with a strap for not knowing his lessons—witness did not have enough food to eat, and often felt hungry.[12]

Augustine, age 7:
Witness had been at the school two years and ran away with Duncan Sticks on Saturday the 8th Feb. Soon after dinner about one o'clock. They had not gone very far when they saw Mr. Fahy [sic] the teacher from the school coming after them. They both ran away and the teacher caught witness and sent him back to the school and accompanied him—Duncan ran into the wood and I did not see the teacher catch him—when the teacher caught me he told me to call Duncan, and I would not. I ran away because the teacher whipped me too much, and because they did not give me good food. Duncan told me he ran away because he was whipped too much.[13]

68

Louis, age 12:
Remembers running away with Duncan Sticks last year.
Someone gave them a ride from Springhouse to Alkali Lake.
They slept the night in a [hay] stack at Harry Felker's [at]
Chimney Creek. Witness ran away because they whipped him
all the time. It was the teacher who whipped him with a strap
on the legs.[14]

The Native men who testified corroborated these reasons
for the runaways. Although some expressed support for the
Mission, all felt the children were being mistreated. However, they felt powerless and afraid to complain.

Johnny Sticks, Alkali Lake, father of Duncan:
"I was glad for him to be at the school. He ran away from the
school about a year ago. . . . He gave as his reason for running
away that he did not get sufficient food and that they whipped
him too much. . . . He was sick when he arrived home and when
he got better I brought him back to school—I made no complaint to the fathers at the Mission about his treatment. I last saw
him alive in July at the school—he seemed well and happy—
the next time I saw him was on Monday the 10th February last
about six o'clock in the evening. . . . He was lying seventy-five
yards off the road in the snow—he was quite dead, but not
frozen. His hat was lying about one yard away, and he had
marks of blood on his nose and his forehead—the left side of
his face had been partly eaten by some animal. I picked up the
cap, and saw marks of fresh blood on the inside, and thought
it came from his nose—the body was then brought on a sleigh
to my house. . . . I received no word from the Mission that any
boy had run away—if I had I should have gone at once and
hunted for him."[15]

Charlie Johnson, Alkali Lake:

"I have a boy at St. Joseph's Industrial School—he has been there four years . . . he has run away three times—last November was the last time & on that occasion he came home—he said he ran away because he was badly fed and beaten—I never saw any marks on him, and made no complaint to the Fathers. I sent him back to school each time he came home. . . . I did not complain to the Fathers about my boys [sic] treatment because I was scared."[16]

John Haines, Alkali Lake:

"I had a girl at St. Joseph's Industrial School for five years—she ran away twice from the School. . . . She told me she ran away because the Sisters gave her rotten food to eat, and they threatened to punish her if she did not eat it—I dident [sic] complain about the bad food because I was ashamed to speak of it. I would not send her back to school when she ran away last time, as I was afraid something would happen to her if she ran away."[17]

Little Pete, Alkali Lake:

"I am deputy Chief of this Rancherie—I was glad when the Government started St. Joseph's Industrial School for the Indians, but think they are not treating the scholars right, when they run away so much—and that ill treatment is the cause of the deceased running away and meeting his death—I have complained to the Fathers that the children must be ill treated, and the Fathers said they were treating them well—that they were well fed and dressed and had a good home."[18]

Several days before the inquest was to begin a priest from the Mission visited Alkali Lake. Father Chiappini presented his version of the events leading up to Duncan's death, and then instructed the people not to speak to any other white people about the boy's death:

John Haines, Alkali Lake:
"I heard Father Capini [Chiappini] speaking to the Indians at the Rancherie [Alkali Lake] about the School. He told the Indians they were not to speak or write to anyone about the school, except to the Bishop or to Mr. Bell the Indian Agent, he said the white men were jealous about the school and wanted to stop it, he said we make nothing out of the school, but lose, because we like to help the Indians, and do what is right for them and the white men are jealous like the devil—he said the white men were trying to stop the Priest from doing good to the Indians—he told us to keep quiet about the dead boy and if any white men tell you anything about him not to do it but do only what the Bishop or the Priest tells you. He said we don't get enough money from the Government to give the children better food."[19]

George Jim, Canoe Creek:
"I heard Father Capini [sic] speak to the Indians at the Alkali Lake Rancherie. He said on the Saturday when crazy Johnnie's boy and Johnny Sticks boy ran away, he said one of the Priests followed the tracks on foot to hunt them—he caught up to the deceased boy on this side of the Mission Creek, and then left him and went after the other boy—he said if you want to write anything to the Bishop, you can write now if you want to say everything good about the School, as the Bishop is sorry about the scholars running away, he said there is no use writing a letter to any other white man, or to speak to them about it."[20]

Evidence presented by the principal Father Boening,

Father Chiappini, Sister Euphrasia, trades instructor Horan, and the teacher Mr. Fahey was relatively consistent.[21] They admitted that the students were occasionally whipped for disciplinary purposes, but the whippings were never "excessive," were never given on their heads, and were always given to students fully clothed. They admitted that the students were sometimes shut alone in rooms for several days in punishment, but they received the ordinary school food and the room was never darkened. When presented with the students' testimony of severe whippings and punishments, Boening remarked that he had heard of these things happening in the past but that was before he took over the job of principal.

The students' testimony of being fed bad food was flatly contradicted. All insisted that the food served to the students was "good and nourishing." According to the sworn statements of two students, both Sister Euphrasia and Father Chiappini had openly admitted to them that there was a problem with the food but had explained that the government did not give the school enough money to provide the students with better food. Sister Euphrasia, when questioned about this testimony, admitted that she had said this but "this was said in a joke."[22] Chiappini, who was in charge of the school's food supply, insisted that the students "get as much food as they can eat."[23]

Why had there been no coroner's examination?
Based on the testimony of Boening, Chiappini, Horan, and a local resident Mr. Rose, the reasons for this failure to examine the body can be reconstructed. On the day after the body was discovered, the principal, Boening, contacted the local Justice of the Peace, a Mr. Hall, who confirmed that by law a coroner should be notified of the death. Later, Father Chiappini himself

went to ask the J.P. about due procedure. At this time Hall informed him that it was unnecessary to notify the coroner, as "the Coroner would not go on account of the distance and expense."[24] By chance, William Thompson, a coroner employed by the province, happened to be at the Mission on the Monday when news of the boy's death came. Trades instructor Horan asked him to investigate. The coroner refused as he thought it was not necessary. According to Horan's testimony,

> I told him I thought it was his duty to hold an inquest, or at least to go and view the body, and he replied, 'certainly not.' He though[t] the Government would not allow the expenses as he could see nothing to warrant an enquiry.[25]

Boening then travelled to Alkali Lake that Thursday to officiate at the boy's funeral, no official examination of the body having occurred.

Why had no one gone after the boy?

A question remained as to why no one from the Mission had pursued Duncan after he ran away. The escape had taken place early in the afternoon, and there were at least four hours of daylight left. It was still winter, and with snow on the ground tracks could be seen and followed. The teacher who had originally pursued Duncan did not follow the boy, but waited until the principal returned to the Mission three hours later to report the runaways.[26] It was not until then that a search was launched. On the principal's instruction, Father Chiappini rode over to Sugar Cane, the nearby village of the Williams Lake band, to inform the people there of the escape of the boys. Some of the men there set out to search, and the three boys from the Williams Lake band were later found. No one had searched in the direction of Alkali Lake, where Duncan had been headed. Principal Boening rode off in pursuit of the four Canim Lake boys who also were caught and brought back. Yet no one attempted to follow Duncan. Boening had simply assumed that without his companion Duncan would return to the Mission.[27] By Sunday the principal began to worry, and he instructed Father Chiappini to "get some Indian" to go look for the boy.[28] Chiappini passed the word to one of the local ranchers that the boy was missing. It was this rancher who discovered the body on the Alkali Lake road later that day. Neither the Alkali Lake chief nor the boy's father had been notified of Duncan's escape.

How had Duncan Sticks died?
Anthony Boitano, a local rancher who discovered the boy's body, described the scene:

> I was returning home, and I heard at the Onward Ranch that Duncan Sticks, a little Indian boy who had run away from the Mission on the previous day was lost—I looked out for his tracks and first saw them where the road forks about two miles below Harry Felker's. There was no other track, and I kept on the road until I struck his track again on this side of the brid[g]e crossing Chimney Creek—I kept following the track which appeared to have been made the night before for about a mile and a half beyond the bridge, until I found the boys [sic] body lying under a tree, about seventy yards from the road. He was lying on his face, and his hat was lying under his face—there was blood on his cheeks and behind the ears, and a portion of one cheek had been eaten by an animal—the body was not frozen stiff, but was quite cold and he appeared to have been dead for some hour—I

noticed some blood on his cap. . . . I turned the body over on its back and recognized it as that of Duncan Sticks.[29]

This description of the boy's body corroborates the description given by the boy's father, Johnny Sticks, who had viewed the body later that day. However, Johnny added some further details: there were marks of blood on the boy's nose and forehead, and there was blood on the inside of the cap. These were the only signs of physical damage on the body.

Judging from the questions directed at the students, a question that loomed large in the coroner's mind was: when and how had these cuts and bruises appeared? The implication was that different scenarios were possible: first, the boy had been whipped and beaten, and then had run away from the school; second, the boy had been beaten by the teacher when caught, but then continued to run after the teacher began to pursue the second boy; third, the cuts and bruises were the result of stumbling through the brush and falling down in his escape.

According to student testimony, there had been no cuts or marks on Duncan's face before he ran away. The teacher, Mr. Fahey, testified that he had never actually caught up to Duncan, but had come within two yards of him and had ordered him to turn back, while he continued in pursuit of the second boy, Augustine. Augustine stated that he had not seen the teacher catch up to Duncan, therefore there was no evidence that the marks had been caused by the teacher.

Coroner Mostyn Hoops examined the boy's body, which had been exhumed on his order after three weeks in the ground. The coroner confirmed facial cuts and bruises, and made the following report:

The body had no bruises or injuries of any kind—the limbs were also free from injury. On the left side of the face on the upper part of the cheek bone, the flesh had been eaten away by some animal, for a space about one inch in diameter. There was a small wound on the upper part of the forehead, about one third of an inch in extent, crusted by blood—small patches of blood were also found over one eye, and on the left cheek, and some traces of blood were found behind both ears, there appeared to be also a slight bruise on the forehead. The wound or bleeding were not sufficient to cause death, and appeared likely to have been caused, by stumbling, or slipping and falling against a tree or rock, but did not appear to have been caused by any weapon. I examined the clothes worn by the deceased at the time of his death, they were all free from traces of blood, with the exception of the cap, on which were several blood stains and a small quantity of coagulated blood.[30]

The coroner concluded that Duncan Sticks had died from natural causes:

Death was due to cold and exposure, from sleeping out at night in cold weather with insufficient clothing and without food or fire—exhaustion from a long tramp over the mountains in the snow was no doubt a predisposing cause.[31]

RESULTS OF THE INQUEST

After five days of testimony evidence was mounting that something was seriously wrong with the operation of the Mission. Particularly troublesome was the conflicting testimony of the students and the management of the Mission school. The Oblates were very worried, enough so that Principal Boening wrote a desperate personal letter to the coroner and the jury before they had officially reached a conclusion regarding Duncan's death. Boening offered to open up the Mission completely to the jury so that they could inspect conditions for themselves:

> In the interests of Justice and in order that you may have full scope in your deliberations concerning the cause or causes which led up to the death of the boy 'Duncan Sticks' of Alkali Lake, an inmate of the Williams Lake Industrial School. I hereby extend to your self and the Jurymen connected in the case an invitation to make a personal inspection of said school. You will be given free access to all parts of said school including general management of the children in our care, Inspection of kitchen, Provisions, Clothing, Bedding, Tuition, Shops, Manual labour, and the files and all other documents even the books of the Institution will be at your disposal.[32]

Despite Principal Boening's letter, the jury, in its final statement, suggested that there was something seriously wrong at the Mission:

> [The jury is] further of opinion that so much evidence having been given by the pupils at the school, regarding corporal and other punishment administered by Principals and teachers, as well as to the quality and quantity of food given to the pupils, that in view of the expressed wish of the Principal in a letter addressed to them during the enquiry which has been filed with the evidence these questions should receive some independent enquiry from the Government, such enquiry being beyond the scope of this jury.[33]

The Indian Agent, the Catholic Bishop of New Westminster, Native parents and children, and the management and staff at the Mission school had provided conflicting views of the nature of the runaway problem at the school. Each of these definitions was shaped by the public and private interests of the parties involved. In the case of the church and government officials, their private interests were consistently masked by public statements designed to show that their relationships with the students, and their handling of the problems at the school, were in the students' best interests.

It was obvious from the number of children running away that students were unhappy at the Mission. The students pointed to two major reasons for their attempted escapes: being inadequately fed, and being excessively whipped and punished. Had it not been for the intervention of some local white residents, motivated perhaps by their own personal interests as much as for concern for the children, the issue over the care being given to the students would have remained a private matter between the Department, the Oblates, and the local Native people.

On initial investigation, Indian Agent Bell claimed that the students had no good reason for running away; rather, it reflected racial characteristics of Indians. It was in their "wild nature" to resist discipline. Bishop Dontenwill of New Westminster echoed these beliefs. These, then, were standard reasons used by both Department of Indian Affairs officials and the Oblates for not only explaining student resistance, but for justifying the need for residential schools: Native peoples, they believed, needed to be "tamed" and "civilized."

In more private surroundings, though, the Oblates had admitted that there was a food problem at the school. Students had testified that the Oblates had blamed federal government underfunding for the poor food situation. The question of who was responsible—the Oblates or the Department of Indian Affairs—was a critical one hovering over the inquest.

When the priests, nuns, and lay teachers at the Mission school were questioned about these statements, they denied the inadequate food situation. Admitting to these problems may well have meant the end of the Oblates' somewhat strained, but nevertheless useful, financial relationship with the Department of Indian Affairs. Department officials would not take well to being publicly criticized; further, they repeatedly had indicated that no more money could be provided to the school. As a result, Father Chiappini and Sister Euphrasia recanted or denied their earlier remarks acknowledging the food shortage and blaming the problem on government underfunding.

During the inquest the contradictory statements of the students and their parents, on the one hand, and the school management on the other, became obvious to the jury. The jury was compelled to suggest that an independent investigation be held. As described in the following chapter, the Department closed the issue during this final investigation by ultimately blaming the students for the school's recent problems.

CHAPTER FIVE

The Government Investigation

INDIAN AGENT BELL'S EARLIER REPORT into the death of Duncan Sticks, a report filed before the inquest began, had by this time been rejected by Department of Indian Affairs officials in Ottawa. Realizing that serious problems existed, that the public was getting wind of the matter, and that Agent Bell had denied the existence of a problem, the Department thought it advisable to once again conduct an investigation of the situation at the school. As one official stated, "the school should not . . . be allowed to go on as it is."[1] The Indian Superintendent of B.C., A.W. Vowell, was ordered to look into the matter.[2] By this time Vowell had obtained copies of the evidence taken at the inquest and the final report of the jury. Armed with this information, he returned to the Williams Lake residential school.

Vowell carried out his inspection of the school one month after Duncan's death and inquest. On the 24th and 25th of March Vowell questioned staff and students at the school. He then travelled to visit the people at the Alkali Lake village on Sunday the 26th of March. Vowell's subsequent nine-page report to Ottawa systematically repudiated virtually every charge that had been laid against the operation of the Mission school in the course of the inquest.[3] Vowell's report, and his careful construction of the problem at the residential school, are explored in this chapter.

ESTABLISHING CREDIBILITY

Vowell began by establishing the fact that he was the most reliable source of information on the situation at the school. His description of his unannounced arrival at the school gave credibility to the "ordinariness" of what he found. The students were enjoying a "good and wholesome" meal and were looking "in the best of health and spirits and most certainly not indicating by their looks that there was any scarcity of food." Next, before he reported on the results of his questioning of the students, he described his relationship with the children. "The children are always pleased to see me, and look upon me as their friend." The implicit message was that the Department could rely on the veracity of Vowell's account. It was implied that the children spoke to Vowell with total openness, and that their answers to his questions were accurate representations of the care they were receiving at the school.

DISCREDITING STUDENTS' COMPLAINTS

Vowell interviewed the students about the food and punishments they were receiving, and about their reasons for running away. He questioned the boys as a group. He also sought out those boys and girls who had given evidence at the inquest, asking them specific questions about their recorded complaints of the school.

Of seven-year-old Augustine, who had complained at the inquest of being whipped: "When I asked him if he was hurt much he laughingly said 'he was not.' "

Of Louis, who had testified that he ran away because of whippings: "[He said] he was not badly hurt, said he had plenty to eat but that a long time ago he was sometimes hungry."

François, age ten, who also had spoken at the inquest, "said he had plenty to eat since Father Boening came to the school."

Of his group interviews: "I went amongst them and asked if they always had as good a supper and if the food was always as good and sufficient and they smilingly told me it was."

BLAMING THE STUDENTS

Vowell then turned to a group discussion with the boys regarding the food provided:

> Upon questioning the boys generally as to the shortness of food it came out that sometimes some one or other of them did not get enough bread; *I asked them if on such occasions they ever asked for more and they said they did not. I then told them that when they did not have sufficient bread they should ask for more and they would get it* and explained to them that many of the boys, as I had been informed, often got more than they could eat, the uneaten portion being wasted; and that in future if the piece of bread placed at each boys

plate was not sufficient that the Father or any member of the staff in attendance, upon request, would give them more; they said that in future they would do so and seemed satisfied. They then after whispering among themselves for a time, said that they would like to get potatoes more frequently at their meals, and that was all they had to ask for. I afterwards in their presence explained matters to Father Boening, both in respect to the bread and to the potatoes, and he said that *certainly the Management would be only too pleased to do what they asked for, and what I suggested, and further that on no occasion had any pupil ever been refused an additional piece of bread, etc., if asked for.* [Emphases added.]

Vowell here attempts to account for the problem at the school by shifting the blame away from both the Department and the Oblates and directly onto the students. If the students went hungry, he suggests, it was their own fault for not asking for more food. This suggestion contrasted sharply with the students' experience, as reported at the inquest, of their relationship with the adults who ran the school. This relationship was founded on strict discipline and obedience, and was enforced through intimidation and corporal punishment. Orders were not to be questioned, rules were not to be challenged, and certainly the amount of food provided was not to be criticized.

DEFINING THE RUNAWAY PROBLEM

Vowell interviewed some of the girls on the issue of why they had attempted to run away from the school. According to Vowell's report:

When questioned as to their motive for doing so, [they] said they had none, merely felt like running away, wanted freedom from the restraint of school discipline and wanted a chance to play with the boys which they never had an opportunity of doing at the school.

Vowell concluded that this was the real reason that so many children had been running away from the school, and he summarized the reasons as "foolish excuses." Once again the problem had been reduced to the innate nature of Indians to react negatively to discipline and constraint. The residential school's civilizing mandate was therefore justified.

SUPPRESSING COMPLAINTS AND JUSTIFYING THE SYSTEM

Next, Vowell reported that he had reminded the students of how everything the Oblates and the government were doing was in their best interests:

Before leaving I told both boys and girls how wrong it was to run away as by so doing they, to a certain extent, disgraced themselves by such bad conduct, and also caused much trouble to their parents, to their kind friends, instructors and guardians, at the school, and also the Government which was doing so much for them, etc. etc.

Vowell was reporting this also for his superiors' benefit. The public image that the Department and the Oblates were working for the benefit of the children had to be maintained if the Department was to keep its credibility.

DISCREDITING THE INQUEST TESTIMONY

Finally, Vowell discredited the reliability of the evidence presented by students at the inquest:

> Touching on the reliability of answers received from Indian children to questions put at random I may here remark that from my own observation outsiders asking questions can seldom really obtain correct answers inasmuch as the children, in most cases, dont [sic] understand exactly the nature of the question put from the fact that they are too timid and dont [sic] pay proper attention, etc. I have known them on such occasions to say 'yes' when it afterwards turned out that they would have said no did they thoroughly understand; consequently, as they are inclined to answer as they think you would like them to, if an outsider wants them to say that such and such a thing is the case it is an easy matter to get them to answer in the affirmative, or vice versa.

Having previously established his status as an insider when he described his warm reception by the school children, the veracity of Vowell's own report, therefore, was reaffirmed.

On the third day of his investigation Vowell travelled to Alkali Lake. Many of the people there were gathered at the village for church services conducted by the local missionary. In this setting, with the church presence looming in the background, Vowell interviewed a number of the adults, who

> ... had no complaints to make about the school, expressed themselves as being sorry for all the trouble caused by the running away of the children from time to time; and promised to do all they could to put a stop to any future irregularities of the kind.

While he was at Alkali Lake, Vowell sought out two ex-students of the Mission school who had given damning testimony at the inquest. The two girls, Christine Haines and Ellen Charlie, stuck steadfastly to their stories. Vowell discredited their charges by pointedly remarking that these girls had been discharged from the school for bad conduct.

MISSION ACCOMPLISHED

In conclusion, Vowell was satisfied with the results of his investigation:

> I would state that the inquiry held will I feel sure to be beneficial in every respect as giving confidence to the children that they are being looked after by the Department and also in letting the Management understand that their actions in the conduct of the school are under close observation, etc. It has also proved highly satisfactory to the Indian for the same reason, and I trust that there will be much less in the way of irregularities to complain of in the future than unfortunately there have been in the past.

What then, had been the purpose of the investigation? According to Vowell's summary statement, there had been two purposes. The first goal had been to convince the students and their families that the students' welfare was being looked after. In short, the investigation had been a public relations job. Second, the Department sought to intimidate the Oblates into running a 'tighter ship.' The Oblates were instructed to provide adequate food, to limit corporal punishment to extreme cases, and most importantly, to exercise greater control over the students so that problems did not get out of hand; that is, come to public attention. The problem was again defined as the lack of discipline at the school.

The Oblates, the Department of Indian Affairs, and the Native parents and students each had their own definition of the problem behind the student runaways. The parents and the students repeatedly pointed to excessive physical punishments, and the poor diet, as reasons for the runaway problem. They did not ask that the Mission school be shut down, but simply that the students be cared for properly.

In response, the Oblates and the Department of Indian Affairs officials collaborated on a mutually beneficial explanation. They told the children that, in the end, it was their own fault for not requesting more food, and for unreasonably resisting the civilizing program. In private, however, the Oblates avoided personal accountability by pointing a finger of blame at government underfunding. Department officials blamed the Oblates for not being able to control the students. Both the Oblates and the Department were able to maintain the appearance of acting in the Natives' best interests while pursuing their own agendas of maintaining the residential school system, maintaining public credibility, maintaining their own policies of fiscal restraint, and ultimately, maintaining the assimilation program. Unfortunately, the interests of the students were sacrificed to these goals.

Even more unfortunate was the demoralizing impact that the investigations had on the student population. Although the students had voiced their concerns at the inquest, their complaints ultimately had been invalidated. Slowly, over the years, many of the students at the Mission school began to accept the Oblates' and the Department's definitions of the problem. They began to believe that it was wrong to resist discipline, and that they were, in fact, an inferior people. By

Christmas of 1903 the process of suppression of the student's voices, and the internalization of notions of inferiority, were evident in the students' Christmas letters to the Deputy Superintendent of Indian Affairs in Ottawa:

Dear Sir,

It gives me great pleasure to write to you and and [sic] to wish you in the name of all the boys of the Williams Lake Industrial School a Happy New Year and many returns. You have been always very kind and good to us but we have been bad. We will try to become better, never to run away from school any more. We will learn our lessons well, we know you will be pleased then with us. The boys are all well. We are now in holidays. We are sliding on the lake every day. I weigh now 74 lbs., on August 4th I weighed only 62 ½ lbs. One new girl weighed only 48 lbs. when she came on July 31st and on September 18th she weighed 58 ½ lbs. We are going to buy skates and many toys from Father with our tickets which we got for studying our lessons well. On Christmas we had a fine time. We got lots of candies. We are all thick and fat. We are respectfully yours the boys of Industrial School.

[signed] Isidore[4]

CHAPTER SIX

Runaways and a Suicide

RUNAWAYS CONTINUE

CHILDREN CONTINUED TO RUN away from the Mission through the first decade of the 1900s. By the autumn of 1910 the problem had become so serious that the boys were barred from working in the fields. Finally the principal, Father Boening, sent a letter to Frank Pedley, the Deputy Superintendent General of Indian Affairs in Ottawa. The principal asked that an official be sent to the school to investigate. He insisted that he had no idea why the students were running away, since neither they nor their parents would talk about the matter. He pleaded:

> You easily understand our pain and our grief at such a state as we are all one mind and one soul to do everything for the children given over to our care . . . we beg you to kindly have someone come here and see the school and the Indians and hold a general inquiry so that these sad dispositions may soon cease.[1]

The principal included in his letter several other letters that students had written to their parents, letters in which the children spoke well about life at the school. These, Boening pointed out, were "good proofs in favour of the school."

The principal had also asked Isaac Ogden, the local Indian Agent, to visit the school, hoping that the Agent would talk to the students and use his authority to try to stop the runaway problem. The Indian Agent, however, was on holiday and unable to visit the school. Ogden did respond, though, with some comments. He suggested that the runaway problem was the Oblates' fault for not keeping a closer watch on the children and for feeding the children inadequately. As evidence of the latter, the Indian Agent noted that he had recently questioned two runaways as they were being returned to the school. Both had complained about the food situation at the Mission.

Principal Boening was irate at the Indian Agent's response. He was especially upset at the Indian Agent's suggestion that the runaway problem was the school's fault. In a subsequent letter the principal defended the school, pointing out that in the nine years that he had been running the school this was the first time that he had asked for the Indian Agent's help in controlling the runaway problem. The principal denied that the Oblates were not caring for the children properly. As evidence, he enclosed letters written by the same two students that the Indian Agent had said complained to him about the food. The principal emphasized that "these letters have not been dictated to them but are their own work."[2] The two children, both from Canim Lake, completely recanted their stories. They did not deny the existence of a poor food situation, but rather denied having spoken to anyone about it. Lizette Theodore, in her letter to the Indian Agent, wrote:

> At the last mail Father received a letter from you in which was said that I had said the food was not good. I never even said or think to say such a thing. Whosoever said so told you a big lie, for I never even speak about it. . . . I tell you thousand times I never think to speak about food nor think of the school when I am at home. . . .[3]

Principal Boening did not stop there, but took it upon himself to clarify the situation at the school to the Department of Indian Affairs in Ottawa. In a letter a few months later he portrayed the Mission as being the victim of "the most absurd accusations," not only from the local Natives and the white settlers, but from "such as we thought friendly disposed, yes, even from employees who knew better," meaning the local Indian Agent.[4] As evidence for "how an innocent word can be twisted" Boening sent along the two students' letters recanting their complaints against the school.

In constructing the nature of the runaway problem at the school the principal once again drew on the notion that Native people could not know what was best for them. "The fact is that the Indians of this agency are ignorant about the purport, the working and benefits of the school. How could they know?"[5] Boening expressed gratitude for any help the Department could give him in convincing the parents to keep their children in the school. In short, he had requested a Departmental investigation of the runaway problem not so much to seek out the roots of the students' unhappiness, but to convince the students that their best interests were being looked after and to intimidate them into submission to the school's authorities.

THE SUICIDE PACT

A decade later yet another tragedy occurred that once again drew Departmental attention to the plight of students at the Williams Lake residential school. In the summer of 1920 nine boys at the Mission grouped together and ate some poisonous water hemlock. One boy, Augustine Allan, died as a result, while the other eight survived. The local coroner was notified, but he did not hold an inquest. He believed there to be nothing unusual about boys eating poisonous weeds.[6]

This event was very disturbing to the boys' relatives. Shortly after the boy's death a Canoe Creek man named Sam wrote to the local Indian Agent and asked that his son Wilfred Basil be taken out of school. Sam complained that the boys were being excessively beaten by the school disciplinarian. The boys who had taken the poison, he said, were very depressed. It had been no accident. Instead, it had been a suicide pact brought on by the excessive beatings that the boys were suffering. Sam asked that his boy be discharged from school before anything else happened to him.[7]

The dead boy's father, Paul Stanislaus from Canim Lake, was deeply grieved at his son Augustine's death. He had not been immediately notified of the death, and the boy had been buried before his father had a chance to see him one last time. His other boy was still in the school, and Stanislaus worried that he too would attempt suicide. Stanislaus was compelled to write to the Indian Agent to ask for his second son's release:

I am asking you to write to Indian Department, to see if I can have my boy out of school. One of them died up there at Mission and they did not send any notice to me to say that he died they wrote and say that he was going to burry [sic] him in the morning. You know how it is for a man not to see a boy of his before the body is put away, so let me know if you write and write me back when you get the answer, the boy I want out is Patrick Allan. Augustine Allan is the one died up there. 7 of them eated [sic] some poison roots and this the only one that died the others were saved. I am afraid this boy might do just the shame [sic] some day.[8]

INDIAN AGENT O'DAUNT'S REPORT

Indian Agent O'Daunt did not believe the suicide pact explanation, nor did he believe that the boys were being excessively beaten. In a letter to the Secretary of the Department of Indian Affairs he reported:

> Indians are very much adverse to any kind of restraint, and to put it mildly, are not to be believed, as a general thing when they complain about Schools or similar Institutions, as they let their imaginations run riot, if they think that by so doing it will help them to gain what they happen to want at the moment.[9]

However, the Indian Agent was worried that a theory like this was liable to "spread like wildfire among the Indians." Given that the matter had the potential for causing a great deal of controversy, not only in the district but for the Department, he reluctantly suggested that, since the Department had been notified, "it would appear that we should take some action to ascertain the truth of the complaints against this 'Lay brother.' "[10]

Although Indian Agent O'Daunt had no reluctance to investigate the allegations of mistreatment of students, he nevertheless believed that such an investigation would be difficult. He suspected that if any abuse was occurring, the Oblates might attempt to cover it up. Rather than conducting the investigation himself, O'Daunt suggested that a medical officer should pay a surprise visit to the school:

> By this means we should know whether boys were unduly flogged as claimed by the Indian, and if the examination was held ostensibly for some other reason, such as to locate possible causes of Rupture etc., the School authorities would not be aware of what we were doing. Should the doctor find no traces of abuse, as I do not think he will, the matter can rest there, and we can ignore the complaint of the Indian.[11]

O'Daunt saw this as the only way to find out what really was going on at the Mission:

> Without a medical examination, to identify boys who have recently been flogged, it will be quite impossible to obtain any evidence as the fear of the Church would keep any youngster from coming forward.[12]

As the children were due to leave on summer holidays in two weeks (August 15), the Indian Agent suggested that the medical exam should be done immediately. He asked J.D. McLean, Secretary of the Department of Indian Affairs in Ottawa, for immediate permission to start the investigation. However, McLean was reluctant to take the step of investigating the school until he was sure there was a problem. Instead, he wanted more information, and he instructed the Indian Agent to send in a "full report" on the matter.[13]

Indian Agent O'Daunt was very frustrated with this reply.

McLean was clearly reluctant to question the integrity of the Oblates. O'Daunt sent back a frank, critical letter to McLean. The "full report" requested by McLean required the medical examination that O'Daunt had requested. Since the students were off on holidays, this examination now was impossible. O'Daunt, though, offered to travel to all of the reserves to collect testimony from the students in the safety of their own homes, and he requested authorization to do this.[14]

The Indian Agent had more to say. Commenting on the difficulty of getting reliable information on what was going on, he noted that there existed, on the one hand, a "great tendency to lying upon the part of the Indians . . . on the other we have a decided lack of something upon the side of the Missions." He did not stop there, and launched a direct attack on the Mission:

> From my own personal knowledge of Mission conditions in the past in other places, the fact that it is a Religious organization of any sort running the place does not by any means place it above suspicion, and in fairness to the poor children who are committed to the mercy of the missionaries for several years of their young lives a thorough and at the same time unbiased investigation ought to be made. To do this properly, without first having medical evidence will be very difficult, as anything I can now find out will be unconfirmed statements of Indian children, against the testimony of the Church authorities, and to take action upon that will bring a religious hornets nest around the ears of the Department, unless the reverence in which missionaries are held in the East has undergone a great change since I lived there.[15]

He went on to criticize the entire residential school system. He argued that the money being provided to church-run residential schools would be much better spent on establishing day schools on the reserves. This way all of the children, instead of just a few, would receive education. Further, the Oblates were taking the entire credit for the operation of the Williams Lake residential school. The day school system, since it would be run entirely by the Department, would have the added benefit of promoting the Department's public image, demonstrating the good job the Department was doing in providing for the Indian people.

THE PRINCIPAL RESPONDS

Secretary McLean in Ottawa remained reluctant to investigate. Instead of giving Indian Agent O'Daunt the go-ahead, he wrote directly to the principal of the school. Informing the principal that complaints had been made about "unduly severe punishment" being given to the students, and noting that severe punishment was something that the Department "would not tolerate," McLean now asked the principal to submit a "full report."[16]

The principal, Father Maillard, responded immediately in a very indignant letter. He was surprised, he wrote, at the tone of McLean's "angry" letter. Maillard had just returned to the school after a year's absence, during which time a Father Duplanil had taken over the running of the school. Maillard insisted that during his absence the school had operated without problems; however, he was willing to tolerate an investigation, as it would, he believed, uncover the source of these "false reports." He concluded that if the Department was not pleased with the way in which he was operating the school that it should notify the Bishop at Vancouver, who would replace him with another principal.[17] That, in short, was the principal's "full report."

THE INSPECTOR'S INVESTIGATION

By this time Paul Stanislaus' request had landed on the Department of Indian Affairs' desk in Ottawa. The issue, it seemed, would not go away. Secretary McLean was still reluctant to send the Indian Agent in to investigate, worrying that O'Daunt's hostile attitude toward the Mission would make the matter worse for the Department. The principal of the school had flatly denied that any problem existed. The next course of action, then, was to notify the Inspector of Indian Schools in Vancouver to look into the matter. Inspector Cairns was asked to visit the school at Williams Lake, and to "inquire particularly into the discipline and punishment meted out by the staff to the pupils of this school."[18] Secretary McLean reaffirmed that severe corporal punishment was unacceptable to the Department. He suggested that Inspector Cairns consult with Indian Agent O'Daunt about the students' complaints about severe punishment.

Inspector Cairns handed in his report in early November. As the school had been inspected that July, Cairns thought it unnecessary to visit the institution again. He did not speak to the students at the school to ask about their concerns. He did, however, meet with past principal Duplanil, who had been the principal of the school at the time of Augustine's suicide and who was now principal at St. Mary's residential school at Mission. Duplanil said that no problems had existed at the school that summer except for one boy who had been "rude" to the disciplinarian. As a result the boy had been beaten. This beating had been an infraction of the school's rules, as the disciplinarian should have notified the principal first. However, Inspector Cairns thought that the punishment had suited the behaviour. The boy later ran away from the school. These had been the only problems that summer, according to Duplanil.[19]

Inspector Cairns also had written to Indian Agent O'Daunt for information regarding the students' complaints. The Indian Agent reportedly had told Inspector Cairns that since the Department had failed to heed his earlier advice on sending in a medical doctor to inspect the children, too much time had passed, and it was useless to investigate further.

In short, Inspector Cairns did "not see that any good purpose could be attained at this late date by an investigation."[20] From the Department's perspective, the matter was closed.

Girls at the mission school, ca 1908. PHOTO: JOSEPHINE BOB

Girls at St. Joseph's Mission on an outing with Sisters of Child Jesus and school principal. PHOTO: JOSEPHINE BOB

The Mission relied heavily on student labour to keep the school in operation. The girls sewed, mended, and washed all of the children's clothing; the boys were kept busy with farm and ranch work and cutting firewood to heat the school buildings. PHOTO: JOSEPHINE BOB

St. Joseph's Mission, ca 1910. Most of the old buildings were destroyed in a fire in 1954, after which time a new student residence was constructed. PHOTO: JOSEPHINE BOB

Girls class at St. Joseph's Mission, 1935. PHOTO: BRITISH COLUMBIA ARCHIVES AND RECORDS SERVICE

CHAPTER SEVEN

History in the Present

B Y THE EARLY 1900S THE NORTHERN Shuswap had adjusted to their changed circumstances. Families continued to support themselves primarily by hunting and fishing. Many families also had begun to grow vegetable gardens, to raise small herds of horses and cattle, and to cut wild hay meadows to provide the herds with winter feed. Although each Shuswap band had a principal village, people continued to move in a seasonal pattern between the reserve village and hunting grounds, fishing stations, winter traplines, and summer gardens and hay meadows. Trapping, the sale of cattle, and occasional employment in packing, freighting, and ranch labour provided families with a bit of cash income. This mixed economy, based on a combination of subsistence practices, sale of locally produced goods, and participation in wage labour, enabled the Shuswap to thrive during the early decades of the 1900s. The Shuswap successfully withstood the Depression years, and the periodic crashes in the fur market, simply by shifting emphasis to hunting and fishing, practices that continued to form the backbone of Shuswap economy and culture.

By 1920 the Williams Lake residential school had been

operating for thirty years, and St. Joseph's Mission for over fifty. Earlier problems between the Mission and local businessmen had since passed, and the Oblates now enjoyed a secure position within both the white and the Shuswap communities in the area. Churches had been built on all the reserves, and priests from the Mission made regular visits to all of the outlying Shuswap communities.

The Shuswap chiefs' earlier struggles to maintain authority in their communities was partially resolved through an innovative alliance with the Catholic church.[1] The Oblate missionaries, in a program known as the Durieu system, sought to establish in each Native village a system of hierarchical administration through which adherence to Catholic morality and values would be strictly enforced.[2] The local missionaries acted as supervisors in the establishment and operation of the village system. The missionaries typically attempted to appoint the hereditary chief of each band to the new position of "church chief." The church chief, in turn, was expected to enforce a strict system of social control within the village. In particular, the church chief was to prevent traditional ceremonies, dancing, gambling, and drunkenness on the reserve, and to encourage the residents' regular attendance at church services. Their authority diminishing as a result of the immense social changes their communities were going through, the Shuswap chiefs took up the Durieu system willingly in the 1890s, remodelling it for their own purposes and effectively implementing the system as a means of restoring social order and maintaining the integrity of their communities. The chiefs regularly held court where, often in the presence of the local missionary, they fined reserve residents for public drunkenness, gambling, and sexual immorality. This system of formal social control persisted in many of the northern Shuswap communities until the 1940s. Like their response to other forces of colonialism, the Shuswap responded to the missionization program with a mixture of resistance and accommodation.

Conditions at the Mission school, however, had not improved significantly since earlier times. Students continued to complain about being poorly fed and subjected to harsh physical punishments. The priests, brothers, sisters and lay teachers at the school, the local Indian Agent and higher officials in the Department of Indian Affairs, the parents of students and students themselves all agreed that there were problems with the school, and that these problems were manifested in the numbers of students running away. However, the various parties involved had different views of the causes of the school's problems.

Previous studies of the Indian residential school system that have portrayed Native parents and students as willing and active participants in the operation of the schools have greatly downplayed the role of coercion in influencing Native responses.[3] To assess Native responses to the schools, the broader context of the relationship between Native people and the church and government needs to be examined. We need to ask: what factors affected Native people and influenced the way they perceived and dealt with problems that arose in the schools? What mechanisms supported or blocked their protests?

In the decades after the establishment of the Mission school Native parents repeatedly protested the care being provided to their children at the school. Yet government officials and missionaries persistently defined the problem at the school not as one of inadequate care, but as the children's refusal to submit to discipline. Why were government officials and missionaries unable to accept the parents' complaints? Why did they define the problem as one of a lack of discipline, rather than one of inadequate care?

The problems at the school were not simply the result of a clash between Native and European styles of child-rearing. The educational philosophy of the residential schools emerged from a European and Christian cultural tradition in which corporal punishment and strict obedience to the authority of adults were standard features of child-rearing. Yet the roots of the problems faced by students and their parents ran much deeper.

Native people were isolated from the rest of Canadian society through their unique structural relationship with the federal government. This relationship was defined and enforced by the laws contained in the Indian Act and by the administrative powers of the Department of Indian Affairs. Any formal interaction with the 'outside' world, and any protests about the care of children in the residential schools, were to be presented to officials of the Department of Indian Affairs, whose mandate was to see to the health and well-being of Native peoples.

The students and their parents were not asking for an end to the residential school system; instead, they were asking that the students receive better care. However, allegations of mistreatment called into question the two fundamental tenets by which the church and government justified their involvement in, and control over, Native peoples' lives. The first was the racist belief that Native people were child-like and primitive, and that they were inherently incapable of making responsible decisions and managing their own lives. The second was the belief that Euro-Canadian society had the responsibility, indeed, the burden, to take care of Native people and to raise them to the level of 'civilization' enjoyed by Europeans. Underlying this second belief was the conviction that the church and government were acting as paternalistic benefactors with only the Natives' best interests at heart.

The church and government took a posture of benevolent paternalism towards Native people. When Native people resisted these efforts, however, this benevolence became aggressive;[4] Native resistance was interpreted as further evidence of their inability to know what was in their best interests. "The fact is that the Indians of this agency are ignorant about the purport, the working and benefits of the school. How could they know?"[5] The students' complaints were blocked through government and church attempts to control and redefine the reality of the events surrounding the student's protests. When it became apparent that the problematic conditions at the school were leaking out into public view, the Oblates took deliberate steps to intimidate the local Native people into silence. In the end, the problem was defined as the unwillingness of Native people to acknowledge their inferiority and submit to the authority of the church and government. This definition then justified the very existence of the residential school: Native people need to be 'tamed' and 'civilized.' Problems with the care being provided to the children were covered up as church and government officials sought to protect their public images and to maintain their authority and control.

Some of the school staff and some government officials may well have been sympathetic toward the children. However, the hierarchical structure of both the Catholic church and the Department of Indian Affairs bureaucracy further contributed to the failure to resolve the problems at the school. The Oblate priests and brothers and the Catholic nuns led tightly controlled and regimented lives, and were expected to be obedient to the orders and requests of higher officials within the church. Their ultimate allegiance was to the Catholic church, and the weight of this hierarchy bore down on them and pressed them into silence. The efforts of one sympathetic Indian Agent to investigate the school were blocked by higher officials within the Department who were reluctant to question the integrity of the church.

Native parents had little control over the residential school. Unlike non-Native parents who willingly sent their children to boarding schools, Native parents typically were coerced into sending their children to the schools, had little power to withdraw them, and could not launch effective complaints against the system. Native children were required by law to attend school, and parents who withheld their children were threatened with fines or imprisonment. Native people did not have federal voting rights until 1960,[6] and consequently in the early decades of the 1900s they had no power to voice protest over unfair laws or government practices through voting in federal elections.

The beliefs about Native inferiority that served to legitimize church and government control over Native people mirrored prevailing beliefs within Euro-Canadian society, beliefs that were the product of European colonialist ideology. Native people were culturally stigmatized in the eyes of the non-Native public, and their complaints would have little chance of being accepted as credible. Native parents had little ability to launch public protests and to gain the support of the non-Native society, especially as these protests were against the government and the church, the two pillars of the dominant society.[7]

These factors made Native people virtually powerless in the face of the conspiracy of silence that was enacted by missionaries and government officials.

This story, however, does not end in 1920. It is not simply the story of the unfortunate deaths of two young boys, or of a misguided educational system that has since been abolished. Rather, that such problems could continue unchecked implicates the entire legal and administrative relationship between Native people and Canadian society. This unique relationship, and the image of Native inferiority on which it is based, continue to define Native-white relations today. While Indian education policies may have changed, and many today agree that the residential school system is an unfortunate incident in Canadian history, the premises that have legitimized the coercive intervention of government and church officials into Native lives still persist.

THE MISSION'S LAST DECADES

By the 1930s the enrollment at the Mission had expanded to over 100 students from the Shuswap, Carrier, and Chilcotin nations. In following years some aspects of school life began to change. A recreational program was added to the students' activities; skating rinks and a gymnasium were built, and hockey and softball teams from the Mission occasionally competed with teams from the white school at Williams Lake. A boys' pipe and drum band was put together in 1944, and in the following decades both boys' and girls' bands performed in local parades and competed in regional festivals. The girls' pipe band travelled across Canada on a sightseeing tour during the summer of 1965, and returned to Montreal two years later to perform at Expo 67.

Despite these changes, life at the Mission continued to run according to a system of strict discipline in which religious instruction remained a central component of the curriculum. Students were forced into submission to the school's authorities through public humiliation and physical punishment. One elderly woman, speaking of her experiences during the 1930s, recalls the two occasions she was strapped:

> One time I was strapped for laughing in chapel. Someone said something to me that made me laugh! The other time, I said something to the Sister. When I went into the class, the Sister was there, calling down the class for something. Calling us "redskins," "chocolate-faces." Finally I stood up and said "What about you—you've got red cheeks yourself!" For that I was strapped on the bum. I got twelve strokes on the hands. Then they locked me up in a closet all morning. It was dark! Good thing I wasn't scared of the dark! They made me kneel down at meal time. For two weeks I had to do that. Kneel down during all the meals. Just for saying "You've got red cheeks yourself!"[8]

One man still recalls the punishment meted out to a fellow classmate at the Mission during the 1950s:

> The way they treated us, they treated us just like animals. And I can still remember this little boy. He's about five years old, and we were outside, we had to unload this truck load of wood. We were passing the wood from one to another, from the truck to the basement. And it was about 15 or 20 below. And the little guy had lost one of his gloves. . . . I don't know how many of us were thinking about this young guy, but he's out in the outside, and

there's other boys down in the basement, and he's crying because he's only got one glove. So when the Brother left, we took him and we put him down in the basement so he wouldn't be cold. And the Brother come along, and he sees this young guy, he finds him down inside packing wood. So he grabs him by the ear and he brings him back outside and he told him "It's your fault that you lost your glove, so you stay out here." And that's something that always bothered me. You know, the cruelty that these people had that were supposed to be looking after us.

A boy attending the school in the 1960s remembers becoming violently ill after being punished for chewing snuff (smokeless tobacco) at the school:

If you got caught with the snuff, there was one supervisor that would make you eat the whole can. I remember this one time I got caught. I had to eat that can of snuff. Well, he just made us. Then he got a spoon and he said, "You should use this, it'll be a lot faster," and then he got smart and he put salt on it, and then made me eat it. And I got really sick from that. I got laid up in bed that afternoon, puking and all that.

These incidents have left lifelong impressions on the students involved, and are but a few of the stories told today by ex-students of the Mission. Although some students have positive memories, the overwhelming majority of students recall their time as a traumatic one dominated by feelings of fear, loneliness, and unhappiness. Students today remember being often hungry, being strapped for speaking their own language, and being taught to feel ashamed of their Indian culture and heritage.

Through these decades the Mission school continued to be

plagued with problems, ranging from an incompetent staff and old and deficient buildings to an inadequate budget.[9] Financial problems continued to strain relations between the Oblates and the federal government. Since the 1930s the Oblates had been warning the Department of Indian Affairs that the school buildings were old and dilapidated, and that the heating and light supply were completely inadequate for the school's needs. A 1945 building inspector's report concluded that the Mission buildings posed an extreme fire hazard. The inspector insisted that renovations would be futile, and that the school either should be shut down or a new facility should be built on the site.[10] Finally in 1954 funding was provided to construct new school buildings and residences. Two weeks before students were scheduled to move into the new facility, fire broke out in the old buildings, fortunately without loss of life.

Developments elsewhere in Canada were soon to have an impact on the Mission school. By the mid-1940s Indian leaders across Canada were lobbying the government to bring about the end of residential schools in favour of non-denominational schools and integration into the public school system. The dismal statistics of academic achievement in residential schools compared with public schools supported their concerns. In 1930 only three percent of Native students were beyond Grade six, compared with the thirty-three percent of students in public schools.[11] In the 1940s, students leaving St. Joseph's Mission at age sixteen on average had only a Grade five education.[12] Under mounting pressure to reform Indian affairs policy, a joint committee of the House of Commons and Senate was struck in 1946 to review the Indian Act. In the course of this study a number of recommendations were made regarding Indian education. The most significant recommendation was that the federal government resume complete responsibility for Indian education in Canada. As a result, the residential school system, with its emphasis on religious and vocational training, slowly gave way to a policy of integrating Native students into non-denominational provincial schools.

The Oblates, who by now operated more than half of the residential schools in Canada, continued to defend residential education and struggled against the integration policy.[13] In an effort to keep the residential school curriculum consistent with changing educational standards, the half-day of vocational training was dropped in favour of a full day of academic studies, a change which was put in place at the Mission in 1946.[14] Provincial inspectors pressured the Mission's teaching staff of Roman Catholic nuns to modernize their educational techniques and to try to "secure a more natural and informal atmosphere in the classroom."[15]

By the 1960s the integration policy had reached the Cariboo. In 1964 the federal government assumed full responsibility for the Mission school, although many of the Oblates remained on staff, and the school continued to be run by an Oblate principal.[16] Native students, after completing Grade eight at the Mission, had the option of continuing on to high school in the public schools in Williams Lake or Prince George. By the 1970s day schools for the elementary grades had been established on many of the area reserves. Finally, in 1981 the Mission school closed, bringing about the end of an institution which has had a profound influence on three generations of First Nations in the Cariboo region.

THE RESIDENTIAL SCHOOL ISSUE

The period between 1960 and 1980 was a time of immense change for the northern Shuswap people. The cumulative effects of cultural alienation, dislocation from their traditional lands and the decline of subsistence practices in the face of an expanding forest industry, and marginalization from the mainstream economy finally had brought the Shuswap to a point of social and cultural crisis. Despite its explicit goals, the residential school system had failed to provide Native children with the skills, knowledge, and confidence needed to integrate successfully into the dominant society. By the 1960s life in many of the northern Shuswap communities was characterized by high levels of unemployment and alarming rates of alcohol abuse, family breakdown, violence, and suicide. In the late 1970s, however, a new period began which has seen more and more Native people achieve sobriety and regain a measure of control over their lives.[17] Most important, this period has witnessed the emergence of a strong Native leadership, a leadership committed not only to addressing social problems within the reserves, but also to examining, criticizing, and remodelling their relationship with non-Native society. It is in this context, in which Native people are achieving sobriety and re-examining their personal and collective histories, that the residential school has become the topic of open discussion.

Focus on the residential school issue was heightened in the late 1980s when, in the course of police investigations into allegations of sexual assault in one of the reserve communities, a number of past students disclosed that they were sexually abused while at the Mission. Criminal charges have since been laid against three Oblates. Two other Oblates, both past workers at the Mission, also have been implicated in students' allegations but have not been charged.[18] In 1989 Father Harold McIntee pleaded guilty to sexually assaulting thirteen boys at the Mission in the late 1950s and early 1960s. In 1991 Brother Glenn Doughty pleaded guilty to sexually abusing four boys at the school between 1961 and 1967.

In 1991, in what has become the most controversial and well-publicized case, six sex-related charges were laid against Bishop Hubert O'Connor. The charges stemmed from reported assaults against Native women at the Mission between 1964 and 1967, when O'Connor was the school principal. O'Connor, who at the time of the charges was serving as the Bishop of Prince George, B.C., to date is the highest Catholic official in Canada to be charged with sex-related crimes. The O'Connor trial began in December 1992. After two days of testimony, however, the proceedings were stayed due to the Crown's refusal to comply with the court's repeated requests to supply the defence lawyer with the medical and psychological records of the complainants. The stay is currently under appeal in the Supreme Court of Canada. The staying of the O'Connor case generated national media coverage and public outrage; to many First Nations people the decision was simply another betrayal of their trust in the non-Native justice system.

While the sexual abuse charges against Oblates have caused St. Joseph's to be one of the most well-publicized and notorious residential schools in Canada, concerns with the negative impact of the residential school system are shared by Native people across the country, from the grassroots level to the highest national political organizations. The residential school issue has united Native people across Canada like no other issue in recent history. In 1991 the Cariboo Tribal Council hosted a national conference on residential schools, a conference which drew Native people from across the country to Vancouver for four days to share their stories of their residential school experiences. In August of 1994 the Assembly of First Nations (AFN), Canada's national political organization representing status Indians, released their long-awaited study on residential schools. Entitled *Breaking the Silence*, the report documents the physical and sexual abuses suffered by students in Indian residential schools, and discusses the social and psychological impacts of these experiences and their ongoing legacy in First Nations communities today. In British Columbia stories of abuse at Indian residential schools continue to emerge. In 1992 the Nuu-chah-nulth Tribal Council on Vancouver Island initiated a study of the effects of residential schooling in their communities. Over a hundred interviews were conducted with past students who had attended a total of eight different residential schools in the province. After two years of study, a 1994 preliminary report indicated that instances of emotional, physical, and sexual abuse were widespread. Largely as a result of these findings, the provincial RCMP announced a full-scale investigation into abuse at all British Columbia Indian residential schools, an investigation set to begin in the spring of 1995.

Both the AFN and B.C.'s First Nations Summit have endorsed the RCMP inquiry. Nevertheless, these and other First Nations organizations across Canada are continuing to call for the federal government to hold a full public inquiry into the operation of Indian residential schools in all regions of the country. First Nations organizations are demanding public statements from the federal government and church organizations acknowledging their responsibility for the abuses that occurred in the schools. Finally, First Nations leaders are calling for both the federal government and the church denominations to provide financial compensation to the victims of residential school abuse.

The response of the churches has been mixed. The Oblate order of the Roman Catholic church, as well as the United and Anglican churches, have offered official apologies for the destruction that the residential schools wrought on Native communities. In their submissions to the Royal Commission on Aboriginal Peoples, the Catholic, United, Anglican, and Presbyterian churches committed themselves to reconciling and establishing new relationships with Native people. Many of the churches have set up residential school committees and have held internal conferences and healing workshops with their Native members to address the residential school issue. Joint meetings between church, government, and First Nations political organizations also have been held to discuss the legacy of the residential schools and future directions for the healing of First Nations communities.

These meetings, however, have not been without acrimony. In 1993 the Catholic Bishops Advisory Committee withdrew from the Assembly of Manitoba Chiefs Residential Schools Working Group, which included representatives from the Anglican, United, and Presbyterian churches as well as federal government officials. In withdrawing, the Catholic delegate cited "an atmosphere of self-interest and manipulation," "vicious attacks on the Catholic church," and a refusal to hear about "the positive experiences and contributions of the residential schools."[19] In March 1993 the Royal Commission on Aboriginal Peoples held a special consultation on residential schools at Canim Lake, B.C. Those in attendance heard past students of St. Joseph's Mission recount their residential school experiences, and were told of the initiatives that the Canim Lake First Nation is undertaking to develop community-based healing programs to address problems of family violence, sexual assault, and other issues that are the legacy of the residential school system. The Canadian Conference on Catholic Bishops turned down the Canim Lake First Nation's invitation to send an official spokesperson to represent the church at these meetings; instead, an observer was sent. The absence of a Catholic bishop was notable, particularly in a region in which the church had operated a residential school for almost a century and had been ministering to the Native population for over 125 years. Shuswap leaders interpreted this absence as only further evidence of the church's failure to take responsibility for the devastating consequences of the residential school program.

Equally disturbing is the general tendency of a number of officials within the Roman Catholic church to continue to defend the residential school system. "They want an apology for taking their culture away from them, for educating them in the white man's way. I'm not so sure I can apologize for that," one bishop recently stated.[20] Oblate historian Thomas Lascelles, in his booklet *Roman Catholic Indian Residential Schools in British Columbia*, offers a view of history in which the negative experiences of residential school students are described as "culture shock," the regrettable but unavoidable consequence of two cultures coming into contact. In a troubling use of animal metaphors—children in residential schools are described as "salmon removed from the water," "eagles whose wings have been clipped," "deer . . . placed in a fenced enclosure"—he evokes an implicit non-Native racism that equates Native people with animals; in so doing he naturalizes and presents as inevitable what in reality were the consequences of a deliberately destructive policy willfully enacted by colonial administrators and missionaries.[21] Paradoxically, he dismisses negative Native testimony of their experiences in residential schools as a distortion of the record, as a reflection of Native peoples' unwillingness to be self-critical, and as "a great injustice to those who gave their lives to the children with a great deal of love in their hearts, and with no thought of the enormous sacrifices."[22] In making these comments, history once again is repeated. Native resistance to the residential school system is rendered invalid by church officials who still struggle to preserve their own self-images as paternalistic benefactors and their own conviction in the moral integrity of their mission.

Assumptions of European superiority and Native inferiority continue to fuel relations between Native peoples and the Canadian state more generally. Although the residential schools have now closed, the legal and administrative structures that enabled the government to create the schools, define the curriculum, and enforce attendance are still very much in existence. The Indian Act continues to exist. The Department of Indian Affairs still takes a paternalistic attitude toward First Nations and insists on overseeing the decision- making of Band Councils in reserve communities. The beliefs persist that Native people cannot make responsible decisions for themselves, and that Euro-Canadian society has the moral obligation to interfere with and direct Native peoples' lives, even if against their wills.

First Nations in Canada are now speaking out about the residential schools, not only to begin the process of rebuilding their communities, but also in an attempt to raise the historical consciousness of the non-Native public. The

Indian residential school issue has the potential to serve as a powerful vehicle for bringing about this critical new awareness of the history of Indian-white relations in Canada. Stories about the residential school system such as those told here about the deaths of Duncan Sticks and Augustine Allan provide concrete examples of how the structural inequalities encoded in legislation and government policy, factors which seem abstract and far removed from daily life, in reality have had devastating effects on individual lives. It is critical for these and other stories to continue to be told, and to be heard with an open heart and mind, if we are to prevent the tragedies of history from being repeated.

Appendix

Opening Address by Chief Bev Sellars, Soda Creek First Nation, to the First National Conference on Residential Schools, June 18, 1991, Vancouver. Reprinted with permission.

I would like to welcome you all to the First National Conference on Residential Schools, a conference that is long overdue. Our tribal council, the Cariboo Tribal Council, sees this conference as an opportunity to educate non-Natives so that they can begin to understand why we, the Native people, have so many social problems. But more importantly we see this conference as an opportunity for ourselves and Natives across the country to gain a better understanding of what we need to do to heal the destruction that has been done to our nations. It will be difficult for many of us who attended the residential schools to talk about our experiences there and how they affected our lives after we left the schools because of the simple fact that they bring back too many painful and unhappy memories. But the silent suffering has to end. It is time for the healing to start, and the only way that will happen is if we acknowledge the past, face it, understand it, deal with it and make sure nothing like it ever happens again.

I would like to quote to you the opening statement from the talk show *Shirley* which aired March 29, 1991 on CTV. It was a statement that sent chills through many Native people in the country because Shirley was describing our lives on television and making public stories that we had talked about amongst ourselves but didn't dare tell anyone else until recently. This was her opening statement.

'A strange man visits you and demands to know where your children are. The next thing you know he grabs your children and drags them away. When you try to stop him, he threatens to throw you in jail. Your children are being forcibly taken to a government-run boarding school far, far away, and you know what goes on there because when you were a child you were forced to go there too. You know that your children will be treated like dirt. You know that they will be told that their family and religion is bad, and you know that when they try to speak their own language they will be severely beaten. You know that there could be sexual abuse, suicide, and even murder, but there is nothing you can do to stop it.

'Canadians may find it hard to believe that all of this actually happened to hundreds of thousands of Canadian children over the last hundred years, and only now are we beginning to find out. And that's because the government, the teachers, the education officials, and the church have all been part of a conspiracy of silence.'

The fifth estate and other television programs did stories on residential schools, newspapers from across the country wanted a story, and a couple of books were written as well. Our secrets were being told and for many of us we were forced to remember in detail things that we had tried so hard to forget but were still being tormented by in our unspoken memories. We all know the horrors that went on in these schools, not only with our generation but our parents' and grandparents' generations as well, and the stories being told now are just the tip of the iceberg.

I was telling an older friend of mine from the Sugar Cane Reserve that I would be doing the welcoming address for this conference and he said to me, "You have to tell our story like it is, don't hold back or make it seem like it wasn't as bad as it actually was. People have to know and believe what happened to us. That's what hurts, when people don't believe what happened." And I guess that's one reason the stories have taken so long to come out. When we did get the courage to tell our stories, people thought we were lying, or even if we were telling the truth, that it must have been our fault these things happened. For many of us we allowed the blame to be placed on us because even though we had no power to stop these things from happening we still felt ashamed for allowing them to happen, and shame is a powerful emotion to try to overcome. We were totally vulnerable at these schools. We, as well as our parents, had absolutely no control over what happened there, and so have no reason to be ashamed. There is no shame in being a victim, and it's time we got rid of the sickness in our souls from carrying that shame.

They say that everyone is born with the potential for success and it is only through life's experiences do we nurture or destroy that potential. Well, for many of us, our most vulnerable and impressionable years, our childhood years, had been spent at the residential schools where we had always been treated like dirt and made to believe that we weren't as good as other people. We believed it because that is the way we were raised at the schools, that is the way we were taught, that is the way we were programmed to believe. Many of us didn't know that we should have expected and demanded to be treated as human beings and not as animals or savages, as so many religious and government officials thought us to be. Our mental, emotional, and spiritual growth was extremely stunted because of the way we were treated. And then people wonder why many Natives still are not even beginning to fulfill their potential in a country that is so full of opportunity.

I have heard some feeble attempts by different people who try to justify the schools and the treatment of the children there. Some of the comments I've heard are that the schools were the salvation of many Native children who lived in squalor and alcohol-ridden homes on reserves, and that the schools provided them with food and safety. I'm sure the residential schools may have provided a small handful of students with living conditions that were better than what they had at home, but many of us that were forced to attend the schools did not live in squalor or alcohol-ridden homes, and we had more food and safety on our reserves than the residential schools could ever provide.

Justification for the harsh punishment in these schools is that discipline had to be fairly firm to help us understand that our ways had to be changed, and that the strap was common those days, even in non-Native schools. I am sure discipline in non-Native schools was firm, with the strap being used frequently, but how many of those non-Native students that were strapped and had the opportunity to go home each night went home with welts on their backs, arms or backside? How many of them were strapped until they were black and blue? How many of them were strapped until blood was drawn?

How many of them today still bear the scars of their strappings?

Another comment I've heard is that the schools were successful and that it is a proven fact because the schools produced the Native artists, Native leaders, and other Native people who are successful in today's world. Today's successful Native people are proof of the power of the Native spirit, and *are not* as a result of the residential schools. They exist in spite of the residential schools. I find it hard to believe that these schools claim to have produced the successful Native artists of today when it was considered a major sin to practice any type of Native culture or speak the Native languages. I find it hard to believe that these schools claim to have groomed children for success when we were not allowed to be normal children. Normal children learn by being allowed to experience life and to explore their curiosity, to make mistakes without being ridiculed. We were not normal children at these schools, we were more like robots, always taking orders, never involved in decision-making of any kind. We were never asked what we thought or even encouraged to think for ourselves. We learned very soon after arriving at the schools not to express ourselves. We got into trouble when we spoke our minds, expressed feelings, or dared to question anything. And on top of all that is the constant message that because you are Native you are part of a weak, defective race unworthy of a distinguished place in society, and that is the reason you have to be looked after.

Added to this is the sexual abuse that so many had to endure, and we know that children who tried to report these sexual abuse happenings got the strap for lying. That to me is not training for success; it is training for self-destruction.

And thousands did self-destruct. If they didn't commit

suicide, they became addicted to anything that would numb or distract the pain—and the addictions only became another thing to be ashamed of.

These schools were so traumatic for some that attended that there are those who remember getting to the schools, but have blocked out from their memories years of their time spent there. They have very uneasy feelings about trying to remember, and do not want to bring those memories back. For these people it is just another way of survival.

Being aware of the problem and where it originates from is the first step to recovery. We have been forced to deal with the residential school issues and we now know that all the suicides, the alcoholism, the very low self-esteem of our people, the sexual abuse, the loss of our language and culture, the family breakdown, the dependency on others, the loss of pride, the loss of parental skills, and all the other social problems that have plagued our people can be traced directly back to the schools.

There are many things that have to be looked at, and we have to find ways of reversing the damage that has been done. We have to reprogram our people into believing in them- selves again. We have to find ways of strengthening the family bonds and reviving the traditional values and culture. We have to find ways of mending the spirits that were broken, and it is also important to remember the younger generation who have not attended the schools but who still display the 'resi- dential school syndrome' as it has been called. The cycle has to be forcibly broken, we cannot allow another generation to suffer from the past programming we received at the schools. Some healing is happening now in a number of communities, but the effects of the residential schools are still very evident.

The schools had such an impact on Native people as a

whole because the majority of our communities were required to attend them. It seems the only ones that didn't attend the schools were the ones who were too sick to do the manual labour that was required, or the children whose parents took them into the wilderness and managed to hide them for awhile, but I think there are very few that managed to completely escape being sent to the schools.

The whole issue of oppression of Native people has to be questioned because it was, and still is today, so very wrong. The residential schools where Native children were kept, sometimes for years at a time, is something we have to examine at this conference. Something else that must be addressed is how to deal with the intense anger and even hatred toward the religious orders, governments, and sometimes even white people in general, when one fully realizes what the residential schools have done to them, when one fully realizes what one has been robbed and cheated of. How do we deal with that?

The solutions to our problems have to come from us, the Native people. Although we want the religious orders and governments to be held accountable for their part in the residential schools, and we will be expecting them to contribute to the solutions, it will have to be up to us to decide how we want them to contribute. We only have to look at our past history and our relationship with the non-Native to know that we can no longer allow other people to try to decide what is best for us. Only we know what is best for us.

Finally, we have to remember the thousands who were so tormented by their experiences and years of being made to feel so totally worthless that they ended their lives. They no longer have the opportunity to try and change their lives, but *we do*. We also have a responsibility to help each other across this country, otherwise all the horrible statistics of our people will not improve, and we will lose many more who do not know how to change the way they feel about themselves. It's time we started living again, and not just surviving, as so many of us did for so long.

Once again, on behalf of my Tribal Council, I welcome you all here to share your experiences and begin the task of rebuilding our nations.

Notes

Unless otherwise noted, all letters cited are from federal government records in the RG10 series, Volume 6436, File 878-1, parts 1 and 2 (National Archives of Canada, Ottawa; British Columbia Archives and Records Service, Victoria).

PREFACE

1 Cariboo Tribal Council, "Faith Misplaced: Lasting Effects of Abuse in a First Nations Community," *Canadian Journal of Native Education* 18 (1991): 161-187.

2 Raymond D. Fogelson, "The Ethnohistory of Events and Non-events," *Ethnohistory* 36 (2) (1989): 133-147; Julie Cruikshank, "Oral Tradition and History: Reviewing Some Issues," *Canadian Historical Review* 75 (3) (1994): 403-418.

CHAPTER ONE

1 The term "First Nations" has become the name commonly used in urban and academic communities to describe Canadian aboriginal people. The term "Native" is widely used in non-urban regions of Canada, and is the common label used by Shuswap people in the central interior of British Columbia to contrast themselves with non-Natives. I use both "First Nations" and "Native" interchangeably. I use the term "Indian" when I mean to evoke the viewpoint of non-Native government and church agents. Finally, I use the term

"white" as a general category to refer to people of European ancestry.

2 Matthew 28:19-20, *The Holy Bible, Revised Standard Version, An Ecumenical Edition* (New York: Collins, 1973).

3 John Webster Grant, *Moon of Wintertime: Missionaries and the Indians of Canada in Encounter since 1534* (Toronto: University of Toronto Press, 1984), 9.

4 Grant, *Moon of Wintertime*.

5 Bruce G. Trigger, *Natives and Newcomers: Canada's 'Heroic Age' Reconsidered* (Kingston: McGill-Queen's University Press, 1985), 229, 331-2.

6 Trigger, *Natives and Newcomers*, 202.

7 John S. Milloy, "The Early Indian Acts: Developmental Strategy and Constitutional Change," in *As Long as the Sun Shines and Water Flows: A Reader in Canadian Native Studies*, eds. Ian A. L. Getty and Antoine S. Lussier (Vancouver: University of Brtish Columbia Press, 1983), 56-64.

8 E. Brian Titley, *A Narrow Vision: Duncan Campbell Scott and the Administration of Indian Affairs in Canada* (Vancouver: University of British Columbia Press, 1986), 1.

9 Grant, *Moon of Wintertime*, 81.

10 Daniel Francis, *The Imaginary Indian: The Image of the Indian in Canadian Culture* (Vancouver: Arsenal Pulp Press, 1992), 46-48.

11 Grant, *Moon of Wintertime*, 74.

12 Ibid.: 82-4.

13 Milloy, "Early Indian Acts," 59.

14 Ibid.: 60.

15 Ibid.

16 John Tobias, "Protection, Civilization, Assimilation: An Outline History of Canada's Indian Policy," in *As Long as the Sun Shines and Water Flows: A Reader in Canadian Native Studies*, eds. Ian A. L. Getty and Antoine S. Lussier (Vancouver: University of Brtish Columbia Press, 1983), 39-55. Over the last century the government agency responsible for Indian administration has taken several different names, most recently the Department of Indian and Northern Affairs. I use the older label "DIA" or Department of Indian Affairs, which is the name used today by most Native people in the Cariboo region to refer to the Department.

17 Tobias, "Protection, Civilization, Assimilation," 45-47.

18 Indian Act, *Revised Statutes of Canada*, 1886, Chapter 43, Section 83.

19 Tobias, "Protection, Civilization, Assimilation," 44.

20 Indian Acts: *Statutes of Canada*, 1919-1920, Chapter 50, Section 3, subsection 107; *Statutes of Canada*, 1922, Chapter 26, Section 1, subsection 107; *Statutes of Canada*, 1932-33, Chapter 42, Section 7, subsection 14; *Statutes of Canada*, 1960-61, Chapter 9, Section 1, subsection 112.

21 Titley, *A Narrow Vision*, 104-6.

22 F.E. LaViolette, *The Struggle for Survival: Indian Cultures and the Protestant Ethic in British Columbia* (Toronto: University of Toronto Press, 1973), 44-97.

23 Tobias, "Protection, Civilization, Assimilation," 47-48; Indian Act, *Revised Statutes of Canada*, 1927, Chapter 98, Section 140 (3).

24 Canada, *Annual Report of the Department of Indian Affairs* (Ottawa: Queens Printer, 1884), XII-XIII.

25 Nicholas F. Davin, "Confidential Report on Industrial Schools for Indians and Half-Breeds," 14 March 1879 (RG10, Volume 3674, File 11,422, National Archives of Canada, Ottawa).

26 Ibid.: 2.

27 Ibid.: 11.

28 Titley, *A Narrow Vision*, 78.

29 Ibid.: 76-77.

30 Canada, *Annual Report of the Department of Indian Affairs* (Ottawa: Queen's Printer, 1889), XI.

31 Canada, *Annual Report of the Department of Indian Affairs* (Ottawa: Queen's Printer, 1895), XXIII.

32 Canada, *Annual Report of the Department of Indian Affairs* (Ottawa: Queen's Printer, 1899), XXXI.

33 Canada, *Annual Report of the Department of Indian Affairs* (Ottawa: Queen's Printer, 1895), XXIII.

34 Canada, *Annual Report of the Department of Indian Affairs* (Ottawa: Queen's Printer, 1897), XXVII.

35 Titley, *A Narrow Vision*, 80.

36 P.H. Bryce, "Report on the Indian Schools of Manitoba and the Northwest Territories," 19 June 1907 (RG10, Volume 4037, file 317,021, National Archives of Canada, Ottawa).

37 Titley, *A Narrow Vision*, 85.

38 Canada, *Annual Report of the Department of Indian Affairs* (Ottawa: Queen's Printer, 1923), 56-58.

39 Jean Barman, Yvonne Hebert, and Don McCaskill, "The Legacy of

the Past: An Overview," in *Indian Education in Canada, Volume 1: The Legacy*, eds. Jean Barman, Yvonne Hebert and Don McCaskill (Vancouver: University of British Columbia Press, 1986), 9.

40 Ibid.

41 Chief Bev Sellars (Opening address to the First National Conference on Residential Schools, Vancouver, B.C., 18 June 1991); Linda R. Bull, "Indian Residential Schooling: The Native Perspective," *Canadian Journal of Native Education* 18 (1991, supplement): 1-63; N. Rosalyn Ing, "The Effects of Residential Schooling on Native Child-Rearing Practices," *Canadian Journal of Native Education* 18 (1991, supplement): 65-118.

42 George Erasmus, Opening comments to the Royal Commission on Aboriginal Peoples' hearings at Canim Lake, British Columbia, 8 March 1993.

43 "Text of the Oblate Apology to Native People," *Western Catholic Reporter*, 26 August 1991, p. 10.

44 Thomas A. Lascelles, OMI, "Indian Residential Schools," *Canadian Catholic Review* 10 (1992): 6-13; Thomas A. Lascelles, OMI, *Roman Catholic Indian Residential Schools in British Columbia* (Vancouver: Order of OMI in B.C., 1990). Also: Bert MacKay, a Nisga'a representing the Anglican Church of Canada (Speech to the First National Conference on Residential Schools, Vancouver, B.C., 21 June 1991); Bishop Remi DeRoo, representing the Roman Catholic diocese of Victoria (Speech to the First National Conference on Residential Schools, Vancouver, B.C., 21 June 1991). Many Carrier women of north-central British Columbia argue that their residential school experience was positive, and they credit the schools for providing them with the skills needed to assume leadership positions in their reserve communities (Jo-Anne Fiske, "Gender and the Paradox of Residential Education in Carrier Society," in *Women in Education*, eds. Jane Gaskell and Arlene McLaren [Calgary: Detselig, 1991], 131-146).

45 It is important to distinguish between intentional outcomes and inadvertent consequences. It is perverse to defend residential schools on the basis of inadvertent outcomes of cultural resistance and pan-Indian unity, particularly when the explicit mandate of the schools was to eradicate Native cultures.

46 Jacqueline Gresko, "Creating Little Dominions within the Dominion: Early Catholic Indian Schools in Saskatchewan and B.C.," in *Indian Education in Canada, Volume 1: The Legacy*, eds. J. Barman, Y.

Hebert and D. McCaskill (Vancouver: University of British Columbia Press, 1986), 88-109; James Redford, "Attendance at Indian Residential Schools in British Columbia, 1890-1920," *B.C. Studies* 44 (1979-80), 41-56; J.R. Miller, "Owen Glendower, Hotspur, and Canadian Indian Policy," *Ethnohistory* 37 (1990): 386-415.

47 Methodological problems also arise when studies of the residential school system are based only on written government and missionary records. It is difficult to reconstruct the motives of Native parents and students, and to determine whether their behaviour was voluntary or coerced, when the full context of their actions has not been recorded, and when we are forced to rely only on the observations of people with vested interests in maintaining the residential school system. This case study is unusual in that Native voices have been written down as sworn affidavits to become part of the archival record.

48 Celia Haig-Brown, *Resistance and Renewal: Surviving the Indian Residential School* (Vancouver: Arsenal Pulp Press, 1988); Basil Johnson, *Indian School Days* (Toronto: Key Porter, 1988). See K. Tsianina Lomawaima, "Domesticity in the Federal Indian Schools: The Power of Authority over Mind and Body," *American Ethnologist* 20 (1993): 227-240 for examples of resistance to American Indian residential schooling.

49 Noel Dyck, *What is the Indian 'Problem'?: Tutelage and Resistance in Canadian Indian Administration* (St. John's, Nfld.: Institute of Social and Economic Research, 1991). Dyck presents a description of these contradictions in the course of an analysis of the historical development and persistence of coercive tutelage in Native-government relations. See also Tobias, "Protection, Civilization, Assimilation."

50 Dyck, *Indian Problem*, 27. This study makes use of Dyck's analytical model of coercive tutelage to explore Native resistance to the residential school system and its consequences.

CHAPTER TWO

1. The following ethnographic sketch is based on James Alexander Teit, *The Shuswap*, The Jesup North Pacific Expedition, Vol. 2, Part VII (New York: AMS Press, 1909). Teit characterized the northern (what he called the "western") Shuswap bands as having a greater degree of sedentism and a slightly different system of social organization than the more southerly Shuswap bands. My description here

refs specifically to the northern Shuswap.

2 Robin Fisher, *Contact and Conflict: Indian-European Relations in British Columbia, 1774-1890*, 2nd ed. (Vancouver: University of British Columbia Press, 1992).

3 Edward Sleigh Hewlett, "The Chilcotin Uprising of 1864," *B.C. Studies* (1973): 50-72.

4 Teit, *The Shuswap*, 463-464.

5 Anson Armstrong to James Thompson, 24 February 1863, in *For Friends at Home: A Scottish Emigrant's Letters from Canada, California and the Cariboo*, ed. Richard Arthur Preston (Montreal: McGill-Queen's University Press, 1974), 328-331.

6 Chief William, letter to the *Victoria Colonist*, 7 November 1879 (British Columbia Archives and Records Service, Victoria).

7 Margaret Whitehead, *The Cariboo Mission: A History of the Oblates* (Victoria: Sono Nis Press, 1981), 13.

8 Ibid.: 35.

9 Ibid.: 55.

10 Jacqueline Gresko, "Roman Catholic Missions to the Indians of British Columbia: A Reappraisal of the Lemert Thesis," *Journal of the Canadian Church Historical Society* XXIV (1982): 59-62.

11 McGuckin to Chief Commissioner of Lands and Works, 12 May 1868 (Colonial Correspondence, File 1047D); McGuckin to Indian Superintendent, 25 August 1877 (GR 494, Box 1, File 37); Grandidier to Powell, 9 July 1881 (RG10, Vol.3583, File 1092), all at British Columbia Archives and Records Service, Victoria.

12 McGuckin to D'Herbomez, 17 February 1878 (Records of the Oblate Missions to British Columbia, Archives Deschatelets, Ottawa).

13 Whitehead, *Cariboo Mission*, 66-78.

CHAPTER THREE

1 Robin Ridington, *Little Bit Know Something: Stories in a Language of Anthropology* (Vancouver: University of British Columbia Press, 1990), 84-99; Scott Rushforth, "The Legitimation of Beliefs in a Hunter-Gatherer Society: Bearlake Athapaskan Knowledge and Authority," *American Ethnologist* 19 (1992): 483-500.

2 Grant, *Moon of Wintertime*, 36. Some historians have argued that whipping was used as a traditional means of social control by Native

groups in the Plateau region of the interior of British Columbia (Margaret Whitehead, *They Call Me Father: Memoirs of Father Nicholas Coccola* [Vancouver: University of British Columbia Press, 1988], 16; Lascelles, *Roman Catholic Schools*, 82). Their argument is based on Thomas Garth's article, "The Plateau Whipping Complex and its Relationship to Plateau-Southwest Contacts" (*Ethnohistory* 12 [1965]: 141-170). Garth's analysis, however, was limited to the southeastern Plateau groups, specifically the Nez Perce, Flathead, Cayuse and Kalispel. Further, Garth argues that whipping as a form of social control was not an aboriginal practice, but diffused to these groups from the 18th-century Spanish Franciscan missions in the American southwest. The Shuswap, according to Teit (*The Shuswap*, 586; also James Teit, *The Thompson Indians of British Columbia* [New York: Knickerbocker Press, 1900], 309-310) did have a ceremonial practice in which an elderly man, with the approval of his family, entered a winter dwelling and proceeded to enact a ritual that could involve whippings. The purpose of the ritual, however, was to encourage children to challenge the authority of the whip bearer. In contrast, whipping as a form of social control had a radically different goal of enforcing submission to authority. Archival evidence clearly shows that this practice was introduced to the northern Plateau groups by Oblate missionaries in the 19th century (see Elizabeth Furniss, "Resistance, Coercion and Revitalization: The Shuswap Encounter with Roman Catholic Missionaries, 1860-1900," *Ethnohistory* 42 (2) (1995) [forthcoming]).

3 See Alice Miller, *For Your Own Good: Hidden Cruelty in Child-rearing and the Roots of Violence* (New York: Farrar, Straus, Giroux, 1983). Phillip Greven discusses biblical justifications for corporal punishment of children in *Spare the Child: The Religious Roots of Punishment and the Psychological Impact of Physical Abuse* (New York: Alfred Knopf, 1991). Ian Gibson's *The English Vice: Beating, Sex and Shame in Victorian England and After* (London: Duckworth, 1978) discusses whipping as a form of sexual stimulation. He includes chapters on flogging in the British grammar and public school systems in the nineteenth and twentieth centuries.

4 Dontenwill to Vowell, 26 February 1902.

5 Vowell to Vankoughnet, 1 June 1891.

6 *Annual Reports of the Department of Indian Affairs* (Canada: Queen's Printer, 1897, 1916, 1933).

7 Vowell to Vankoughnet, 1 June 1891.
8 Whitehead, *Cariboo Mission.*
9 Lejacq to Vowell, 5 June 1893.
10 Deputy Superintendent General of Indian Affairs to Vowell, 16 June 1893.
11 Johns to Vowell, 4 November 1893.
12 Robin Skelton, *They Call it the Cariboo* (Victoria: Sono Nis Press, 1980), 84, 194-95.
13 Canada census, 1901, Province of British Columbia, District of Yale and Cariboo, Williams Lake subdivision (Reel B-11275, British Columbia Archives and Records Service, Victoria).
14 Teit, *The Shuswap,* 464.
15 Davison to Barnard, 21 May 1894.
16 Deputy Superintendent General of Indian Affairs to Daly, 19 June 1894.
17 Superintendent General to Secretary McLean, 14 April 1899.
18 McLean to Vowell, 19 April 1899.
19 Vowell to McLean, 24 May 1899.
20 Bell to Vowell, 12 May 1899; Vowell to McLean, 24 May 1899.
21 Vowell to McLean, 24 May 1899.
22 Ibid.
23 Carew-Gibson to Vowell, 23 July 1900.
24 Peytavin to Vowell, 15 August 1900; Bell to Vowell 14 October 1900.

CHAPTER FOUR
1 Bell to Vowell, 28 February 1902.
2 Dontenwill to Vowell, 26 February 1902.
3 Ibid.
4 Ibid.
5 Private letter, Bell to Vowell, 28 February 1902.
6 Ibid.
7 Ibid.
8 Inquisition Report into the Death of Duncan Sticks.
9 Sworn Information of Ellen Charlie, 28 February 1902, Alkali Lake.
10 Sworn Information of Christine Haines, 28 February 1902, Alkali Lake.
11 Sworn Information of Mary Sticks, 28 February 1902, Alkali Lake.
12 Sworn Information of Francois, 3 March 1902, 150 Mile House.

13 Sworn Information of Augustine, 3 March 1902, 150 Mile House.
14 Sworn Information of Louis, 3 March 1902, 150 Mile House.
15 Sworn Information of Johnny Sticks, 28 February 1902, Alkali Lake.
16 Sworn Information of Charlie Johnson, 28 February 1902, Alkali Lake.
17 Sworn Information of John Haines, 28 February 1902, Alkali Lake.
18 Sworn Information of Little Pete, 28 February 1902, Alkali Lake.
19 Sworn Information of John Haines, 28 February 1902, Alkali Lake.
20 Sworn Information of George Jim, 28 February 1902, Alkali Lake.
21 Sworn Information of Sister Euphrasia, Henry Boening, J.D. Chiappini, Joseph Fahey, and Henry Horan, 3-4 March 1902, 150 Mile House.
22 Sworn Information of Sister Euphrasia.
23 Sworn Information of J.D. Chiappini.
24 Sworn Information of Henry Boening.
25 Sworn Information of Henry Horan.
26 Sworn Information of Joseph Fahey.
27 Sworn Information of Henry Boening.
28 Ibid.
29 Sworn Information of Anthony Boitano, 1 March 1902.
30 Sworn Information of Mostyn Hoops, 4 March 1902, 150 Mile House.
31 Ibid.
32 Boening to Hoops, 3 March 1902.
33 Inquisition Report into the Death of Duncan Sticks.

CHAPTER FIVE
1 Brusen to Secretary, 12 March 1902.
2 McLean to Vowell, 13 March 1902.
3 Vowell to Secretary, 14 April 1902. All following quotes in this chapter, unless otherwise indicated, are from this letter.
4 Isidore to Deputy Superintendent General of Indian Affairs, 27 December 1903.

CHAPTER SIX
1 Boening to Pedley, 6 September 1910.
2 Boening to Ogden, 20 September 1910.
3 Theodore to Ogden, 18 September 1910.
4 Boening to Secretary, 8 January 1911.

5 Ibid.
6 O'Daunt to Secretary, 1 August 1920.
7 Ibid.
8 Stanislaus to O'Daunt, 22 August 1920.
9 O'Daunt to Secretary, 1 August 1920.
10 Ibid.
11 Ibid.
12 Ibid.
13 Secretary McLean to O'Daunt, 9 August 1920.
14 O'Daunt to Secretary, 16 August 1920.
15 Ibid.
16 McLean to Principal Maillard, 24 August 1920.
17 Maillard to Secretary, 31 August 1920.
18 MacKenzie to Cairns, 5 October 1920.
19 Cairns to MacKenzie, 7 November 1920.
20 Ibid.

CHAPTER SEVEN

1 Furniss, "Resistance, Coercion and Revitalization."
2 Edwin Lemert, "The Life and Death of an Indian State," *Human Organization* 13 (1954): 23-27; Whitehead, *Cariboo Mission*, 93-106, 130-31.
3 Gresko, "Early Catholic Indian Schools"; Redford, "Attendance at Residential Schools"; Miller, "Owen Glendower."
4 James Smart, Deputy Superintendent General of Indian Affairs in 1898, believed that a course of "benevolent aggression" should be used to enforce Native compliance with departmental policies when efforts at persuasion had failed. *Annual Report of the Department of Indian Affairs* (Ottawa: Queen's Printer, 1898), xxvi.
5 Boening to Secretary, 8 January 1911.
6 H.B. Hawthorn, ed., *A Survey of the Contemporary Indians of Canada, Volume 1* (Ottawa: Queen's Printer, 1966), 260.
7 As in this case, exceptions could occur if the local non-Native public had vested interests in criticizing the government or church.
8 I recorded these three stories in the course of research on the residential school issue with the Shuswap people of Soda Creek in 1992 and 1994.
9 Father Alex Morris (CBC Television's *The fifth estate* program on St. Joseph's Mission, entitled "Violation of Trust," aired in 1991).

10 RG10, Volume 6436, File 878-1, Part 3.

11 Jean Barman, Yvonne Hebert, and Don McCaskill, "The Legacy of the Past: An Overview," in *Indian Education in Canada, Volume 1: The Legacy*, eds. Jean Barman, Yvonne Hebert and Don McCaskill (Vancouver: University of British Columbia Press, 1986), 9.

12 RG10, Volume 6437, File 878-2, Parts 1 and 2.

13 H.B. Hawthorn, ed., *A Survey of the Contemporary Indians of Canada, Volume 2* (Ottawa: Queen's Printer, 1966), 56-58.

14 Whitehead, *Cariboo Mission*, 133.

15 RG10, Volume 6436, File 8778-1, Part 3.

16 Whitehead, *Cariboo Mission*, 135.

17 For a discussion of these events in one reserve community see Elizabeth Furniss, "A Sobriety Movement among the Shuswap Indians of Alkali Lake" (M.A. thesis, University of British Columbia, 1987).

18 Bob Grinstead, testimony to the Royal Commission on Aboriginal Peoples, 8 March 1993, Canim Lake, B.C.

19 "Manitoba church, Native leaders struggle for 'a true path,' " *Catholic New Times*, 7 November 1993, 16.

20 Hubert O'Connor, (CBC Television's *The fifth estate* program entitled "Violation of Trust," 1991).

21 Lascelles, *Roman Catholic Schools*, 4, 19.

22 Ibid.: 5, 82-83.

Index